STORES AND SHOPPING CENTERS

STORES
AND
SHOPPING CENTERS

Edited by

JAMES S. HORNBECK, AIA
SENIOR EDITOR, *Architectural Record*

An Architectural Record Book

McGRAW-HILL BOOK COMPANY, INC. / *New York   Toronto   London*

PREFACE

In creating up-to-date buildings for retailing, the architect and his consulting engineers must deal with a much more complex set of requirements and circumstances than those of a few years ago. Retailing has become a carefully researched science, practiced mainly by "pros"; and the techniques of its specialists have become an important factor in the design of stores.

The store on Main Street—so familiar to us in our youth—has disappeared entirely or is fighting for its life in competition with a knowing, aggressive counterpart in that new shopping center on the edge of town, where free parking abounds. The big department store has changed too; it no longer consists of acres of aisles in military alignment, but is now divided into a series of shops. Each of these shops has an identity of its own and is in scale with its function; and here one can pick up and examine the merchandise that used to be glass enclosed, or even hidden away in drawers or cabinets!

We find that much is being done to make shopping a pleasant experience, since attractive surroundings draw more trade. Gay and compelling forms and colors beguile the eye; artful lighting is playing an increasingly important role; air conditioning is a must; flowers, planting, fountains, sculpture, and benches for the footweary provide amenity in the new market place.

Architectural Record has followed and reported the latest developments in the design of stores and their interiors, as well as shopping centers, both suburban and urban. This book brings together in one handy volume the fruits of that editorial effort, and we hope it will serve to replace the usual disorderly accumulation of tearsheets, back issues, and clippings as a compact and orderly reference to the latest and best in store and shopping center design.

There is wide variety in these examples—variety of size, type, structure, situation, and attitude—and thus a variety of information useful in solving a wide range of problems. There is—perhaps paradoxically—also the common thread of good design that runs through and unites all these examples, despite their variety.

This is a collection·of successful stores and shopping centers; successful as commercial architecture that pleases the eye and profits the owner. The multitude of lessons to be learned and ideas to be absorbed from the words and pictures in this book recommend it to the developers, retailers, architects, engineers, and builders concerned with the buildings and centers for retailing—as well as students of the field.

James S. Hornbeck

v

CONTENTS

SHOPPING CENTERS

STORES AND SHOPPING CENTERS

Robert Doisneau

STORES

Stores are for Merchandising

A store—the most commercial of commercial buildings—must be conceived, arranged, and designed to sell goods; and if it fails in this requirement it has no reason to exist. The fact that a store is built to make money in no wise precludes the possibility that it can also be well designed architecturally. Contrariwise, one can hardly expect a perfect gem of store design to entice visitors into buying merchandise on the basis of esthetic appeal alone. The ultimate store, like the girl who has both beauty and brains, will combine both qualities.

Knowing these facts, the architect—and others interested in stores—can benefit from some knowledge of the nature of retailing, and of how merchandising principles and practices can influence the location and appearance of retail establishments. This interrelationship is discussed at some length by William T. Snaith, in the article immediately following.

In this section's second article—pages eleven to thirty—architect Morris Ketchum, Jr. delves into the influences that the environment, be it urban, suburban, or rural, brings to bear on the design of shops.

Most of this section is devoted to a portfolio of twenty stores —large and small in size—which have in common the quality of good design. Each serves also to illustrate at least one—or several—of the discussed principles at work.

– J.S.H.

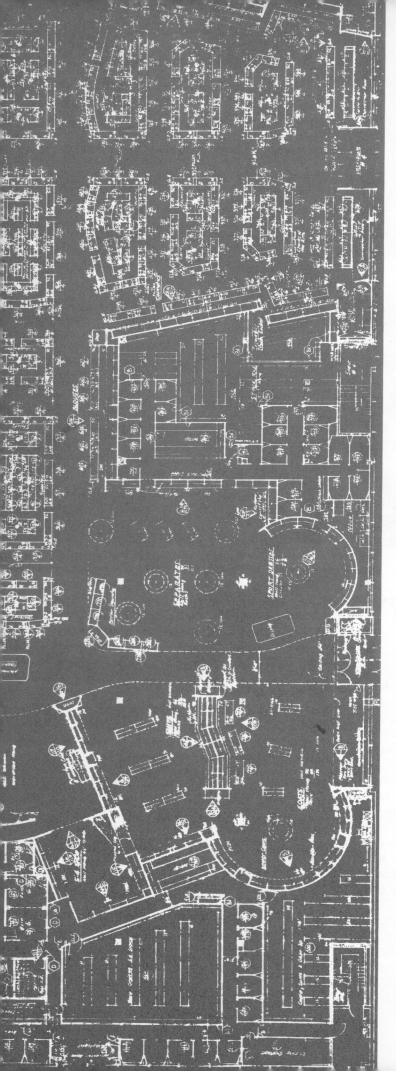

HOW RETAILING PRINCIPLES AFFECT DESIGN

*by William T. Snaith**

THE NATURE OF RETAILING

To design a store—any kind of store—one must visualize a complex and dramatic exhibition combined with the most efficient and workmanlike of warehouses. Add to this diverse pair the knowledge that from hour to hour through any typical day both exhibit and warehouse must be raided and replenished without any obvious public dislocation of the main show. Further, for every type of retail enterprise there is a unique, appropriate solution in building design, interior arrangement, and interior design.

Retailing is a large community, and is neither static nor well-mannered. Within this community the keenest competition exists, and there are no rules to limit the amount of ingenuity, energy, or money any retailer may expend, or to govern the manner in which he may employ them.

There are two extremes of retailing in this community. First, the retailers who sell merchandise by projecting their own personalities; second, the retailers who, in effect, act as distributors of manufacturers' goods and personalities. This is the basic cleavage, and every type in between is a shading of one extreme or the other. The extreme example of the store that sells its own personality is the specialty shop (Tiffany, Sulka). Here, fashion is sold with or without the maker's label—often under the shop's own label. The other extreme is the supermarket shelf displaying dry groceries and drugs,

*Architect Snaith is president of Raymond Loewy/William Snaith, Inc., and qualifies—through years of study and experience—as an expert in the fields of merchandising as it influences store design. In this capacity he has served as a consultant to Lord & Taylor, Stewart's, Foley's, Rich's, Filene's, J. L. Hudson, and many others.

The total impression of fashion store: air of spaciousness; elegant fixtures; off-white, gold, sepia, bronze, sand carpet, pink marble. The J. W. Robinson Store, Beverly Hills, Cal.

where items are selected on the basis of the manufacturer's name and reputation. Such shelves are simply convenient pick-up points for wanted or convenience goods. Approximately 200 billion, 2 million dollars worth of goods are sold yearly in the United States. The solutions for receiving, handling, housing, and displaying this vast quantity of merchandise cannot follow similar principles in each case; the *character* of the particular store must be a basic design determinant.

Currently, the problem of store design is complicated by a very real revolution in total distribution. There is increasingly less distinction in merchandise itself, while the desire and means to acquire goods is growing. People want more of everything; and they want to derive status from their possessions. As retailing reaches the point where there are many places to buy like goods; when advertising encounters increasing difficulty in conveying impressions of differences in merchandise; then the store itself becomes a potent factor for buying in one place rather than another. The skill of a designer is demonstrated in the successful interpretation of a store's special character. It is not demonstrated in an esthetic architectural statement, although this possibility is not ruled out.

An interesting peculiarity of current retailing: two kinds of stores at the extreme of selling for price—the supermarket and the discount house—are being forced to explore the potential of establishing personality and offering some service. Price alone is no longer the compelling incentive it once was; the competitive advantage of these stores is waning.

We shall discuss the effect of a building's design on a retail enterprise. Briefly, these are the main factors involved: geographical location; use of site; interior relationships of operating elements; type of merchandise; exterior and interior atmosphere which projects the store's character. For clarity, the subject will be confined to new buildings. Although modernization is a vast field, the limitations of an existing plant automatically control planning, and improvisation is employed rather than principles of store planning in their most ideal application.

GEOGRAPHICAL LOCATION

Most new retail building is suburban and of two kinds: branch stores in developing residential communities, or units in shopping centers. As a planning exercise, let us analyze the branch unit of a downtown department store, for in no other enterprise are all the design skills so rigorously demanded or so directly measured against profit. New downtown stores are rare, and their locations depend more on possibility than on choice.

In order to appreciate the problem of locating a branch, it is necessary to understand the nature and strengths of a complete department store downtown. This powerful retailing instrument: 1, is located in the major traffic area; 2, is important in the downtown community; 3, is a place in which to look and learn and buy rather than one where only convenience goods are available; 4, offers the widest assortment of merchandise under one roof of any type of retailing outlet; 5, has resources and organization that enable it to buy better than other types

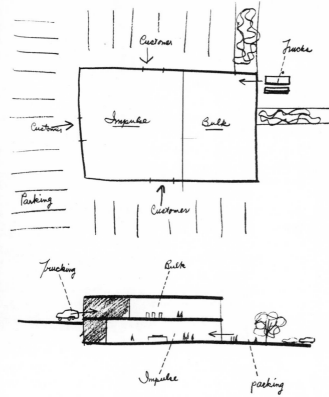

Two examples of two-level parking. At top, parking adjacent three separate entrances; bottom, the split-level plan arranged so the strips in front are filled first, giving the center an active look. Overflow parking in both cases is at the rear. Top: Lord & Taylor, Milburn, New Jersey. Bottom: Stewart's, Baltimore, Md.

Sketches to show proper interrelationship of trucking, bulk and impulse merchandise, entrances, and parking. The plan is for a single level arrangement; the section relates these elements in split-level fashion for a sloping plot or one that can be adapted to a two-level scheme

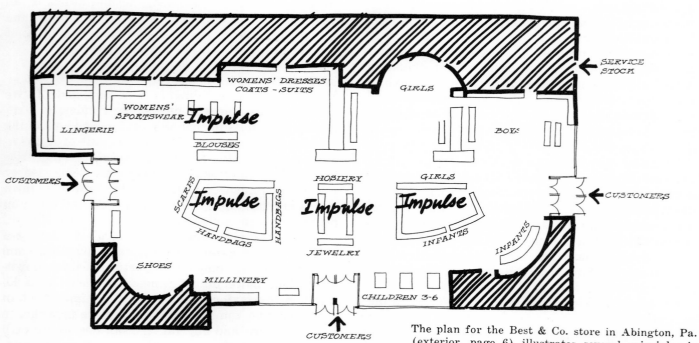

 = STOCK AREAS

The plan for the Best & Co. store in Abington, Pa. (exterior, page 6) illustrates several principles in action. Note the sequence of merchandise (as per text, page 7) and the modified peripheral plan arrangement for the articulation of delivery, merchandise, and internal circulation

of retail stores; 6, has prestige in name and manner of selling; 7, represents community interest beyond the sale of goods; 8, offers service, deliveries, charge accounts, guarantees, returns, repairs, food, facilities, etc.; 9, arbitrates fashion, insuring taste and acceptance for its customers; 10, is a central base for marketing tests; 11, is the focal point for advertising and public relations interpreting the store's special character. This is the highly developed organism which now seeks new outlets to serve its customers closer to home.

The leading department store in a given city runs the greatest chance of injuring its downtown business by branches; the second and third stores have less to fear. But location choice is based—emphatically—on analyzing the position of the proposed store and downtown store in relation to what it considers its total potential. There are two possible locations: close to the city where the branch taps existing customers, or further out where there are new customers. A branch cannot go too far from the main store because the store's range of influence is limited by custom and knowledge. Records of charge accounts and deliveries tell a store where it is doing business. Branch locations are sought:
1. In areas where people are not being served.
2. Where defense against competition is needed.
3. In a new area which is not being served.
4. In a satellite town in case the store's reputation will be able to carry across a wide gap. Bloomingdale's is successful in Stamford; L. S. Ayres of Indianapolis does well in Lafayette; Rich's of Atlanta prospers in Knoxville.

Other factors are physical. Consider accessibility. Although thousands of cars may pass every hour, high speed, limited access roads hardly provide the kind of traffic that will stop to shop. The rules of retailing never change: can customers get to the store? can they stop? can they see the store? Besides accessibility, land must be available in the right place and priced fairly. Obviously, zoning laws must be favorable or changeable.

USE OF THE SITE

Accessibility from the road is the first factor in deciding how to use the site. Next, topography will influence the kind of building, the number of floors, the levels of parking. These will, in turn, determine the kinds of merchandise within the store. Contrary to every traditional architectural dictum that building design is conditioned by the land, no store site must be able to dictate a bad positioning of the building in terms of retailing. Rather, the topography might be changed to achieve a proper entrance or to locate services to work with inside operation. If the site cannot be accommodated to store requirements it must be rejected, however beautiful for esthetic reasons.

PARKING is a prime factor in site use. The store must decide whether it is better to show extensive parking or to show the store itself. The accepted size for parking facilities is based on shopping population. We allow 4 sq ft of parking to one of store. However, the distribution of required area into lots or into a front or rear plaza depends upon the impression the store wants to convey. I like a large parking area less than lots distributed about the store, since a lot is filled only at peak hours. An empty lot gives a not-so-busy impression, which is not good.

PLACEMENT OF THE BUILDING. There is no absolute front for a branch store. Fronts are regarded as facing on streets, or traffic. Instead, consider a branch store as having two "fronts:" one that a customer sees in passing or arriving, the other he sees when he actually enters. Topography may or may not dictate the location of auxiliary services, but such services must back up into merchandise within the store. When one knows where the trucks arrive, he has automatically determined the location of certain departments. These are: bulk goods (furniture, rugs, appliances, etc.); and fragile goods (china, glass, lamps, etc.) which ask for the least amount of handling.

Note that the conventional ideas of locating a building on a site cannot always be applied to stores, for when the truck approach is determined, the location of certain merchandise also is. If, for other reasons, merchandise location is determined first, then there is an enforced location for trucking. We more often create sites than accommodate to them; not arbitrarily, but for very sound merchandising reasons. The designer must determine where the greatest number of customers will arrive, and will then know the level and entrance at which to place impulse merchandise—as we will see later.

SPACE PLANNING

As acutal drawing begins, two major principles are carried in tandem: how the building operates most efficiently, and how it addresses itself to the customer. How does a store address a customer? It conveys an impression of a fashion store (Lord & Taylor), an institution (Lazarus, Columbus), or a store with maximum stock (Gimbels, New York). Many of the great department stores try to do all three, but a single impression usually prevails. We can explain this only by explaining the retailer himself. He is an individualist; he knows how to sell (and does so almost automatically) in one merchandising category better than others, or in one price range, or by one promotional device. The store must address its particular customer, for no matter how intelligent the plan, how appealing the design, this retailer will be unable to do *his* kind of business without *his* kind of store.

Next, a store addresses itself to the customer by the manner in which it presents merchandise; and finally, by the sequence of its merchandise.

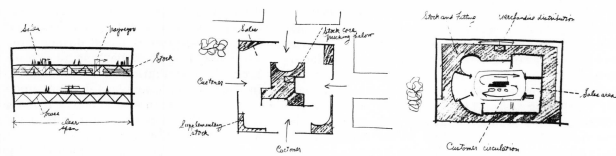

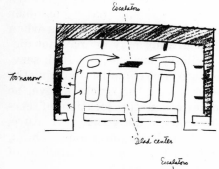

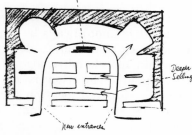

The three sketches above illustrate the three basic arrangements of service and circulation. At left, the sandwich scheme; center, the internal service core; right, the peripheral service belt with central customer circulation. See text at right

Above, an unfortunate (top) and improved (bottom) diagram-plan for the placement of entrances and their working relationship with internal circulation, as well as the size and shape of selling areas in conjunction with both

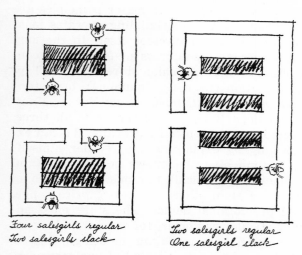

"Station selling consists of an island; customer outside, salesgirl inside. Two islands mean two girls—or more often four, since two sides must be watched and served." One island performs for two in the sketch above

A series of sketches showing exterior design development for Best & Co. in Abington, Pa. Early ideas of peaked roof and overhangs were discarded in favor of more economical canvas marquee shelters. Fieldstone ties in with the domestic architecture typical of this predominantly residential section

Gottscho-Schleisner

ORDER OF MERCHANDISE. Merchandise has a descending order of importance according to frequency of sale and relationship to total impression. First is impulse merchandise, that which is in constant demand and which attracts customers simply by visual or tactile contact. In a department store the items most frequently in demand are smallwares (gift items) or fashion accessories (jewelry, handbags, cosmetics). Next, in terms of placement, is merchandise which gives the impression the store wants to create. Without exception, there is a relationship between this and the impulse merchandise. Here are accessories and fashion apparel augmenting the impulse items (millinery, shoes, sportswear, others). In descending order is the traditional or expected merchandise of a department store, such as stationery, men's furnishing, notions, etc., which rounds out the impression of a total department store. The retailer may want to capitalize on two impressions (fashion and institutional), and if so, he can create two levels, giving each floor its own character. (First floor fashion—Rich's, Knoxville; institutional impression—Gimbel's first floor.)

There is also an order of merchandise imposed by operation. Handling goods spells the difference between an expensive and an inexpensive operation. Reducing the number of handlings increases profit. Most expensive to handle is bulk or fragile merchandise—a determinant in locating delivery approaches, as mentioned earlier.

The third decisive factor is the very nature of a branch store, which is a reduced representation of the downtown store. Thus, if the city store has built a reputation for housewares, there must be a prominent housewares department in the branch, for customers will expect it. There cannot be a difference between downtown store and branch—compression must not destroy essential character. Nor can the planner reproduce a miniature downtown store based on percentages, for some departments would be ridiculously small. Here, statistical analyses break down, and local demands must govern.

If you can't have everything: 1, cut out merchandise having low frequency of sales and low profitability; 2, cut out departments the community will not support, or which—for geographical reasons—are difficult or expensive to stock.

SERVICES comprise: 1, stock to back up a department; 2, sale consummation (taking cash, writing charges, keeping records, packing, delivery); 3, administration; 4, sales personnel. Every store devotes from 25 to 40 per cent of its space, including stairs, boiler room, etc., to such functions.

The size and shape of a department may reduce operating costs and enable the store to offer its best service with fewer sales persons—a major expense item. Station selling consists of an island; customer outside, salesgirl inside. Two islands mean two girls —or more often four, since two sides must be watched and served. If the designer wants to cut personnel by eliminating islands, then he must note that over-elongated shapes, or those that turn (making it optically impossible for a single person to control an area) are undesirable.

CIRCULATION of two types, horizontal and vertical, must perform for both service and customer. Though one elevator penthouse for both would be cheaper, we never hesitate to build two, since a better functional relationship outweighs installation cost.

There are three ways to locate service areas in relation to circulation: 1, sandwich service; 2, internal service; and 3, peripheral service. I know of only one example of the "sandwich" service floor— the May Co. in St. Louis. Of the internal service type, the most outstanding is the J. L. Hudson branch at Northland.

All things considered, the peripheral arrangement is best. It gives separate shop distinction to each department and offers the visual impression of a total floor. The central service block offers only separation by shop, while the peripheral plan allows both. No one has yet built a sandwich floor arrangement that achieves both objectives. The peripheral plan produces the following situation: customer circulation is centralized and also spreads out, while service circulation comes from outside in, and the two types never cross. With circulation decided, site use is reconsidered.

ENTRANCES are located to provide maximum exposure of high impulse merchandise, supported by sufficient surrounding area so departments function well; and proper relationship to most of the parking area.

By presenting considerations in the wrong order— site before space planning—we see clearly the essential difference in the approach of a store planner and the traditional architectural one. The building has not been located on the site until inside space arrangement has been crystallized.

ALLOCATION OF DEPARTMENTS. Two factors affect department allocation: 1, size; and 2, relationship with other departments on the basis of goods, character, and service. Certain departments might be related because of use association, total impact impression, or price association.

In any consideration of space allocation the designer must also recognize that there are seasonal peaks in all selling. 20 per cent of total volume is done in December. So, in the allocation and association of departments one must consider how they complement one another during peak season. Coats and suits and sportswear departments must be designed so they can capitalize on the sale of bathing suits and active sportswear when the weather changes. Toys and summer furniture departments are usually related, because both are bulky stocks, highly seasonal in appeal, and require comparable space.

In a shopping center, the branch department store should stand apart visually. Above, Halle Bros. in Westgate, Ohio, is made distinctive by peaked roof, white brick, and decorative black iron medallion

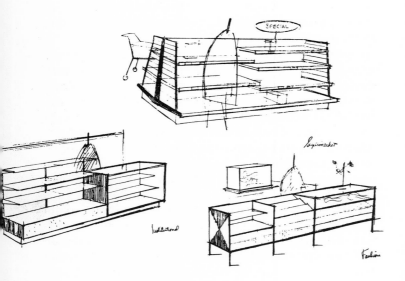

Above, the designer's rendering for a department and a photo of the department. The object is to project the total store image or character to the customer; the kind of merchandise, the way it is sold, the type of customer, the store itself in relation to others handling like merchandise

"In fixture design we must seek some comfortable median between turning the store into a supermarket (maximum self-service) or a salon, where the customer is individually helped at every stage of the sale." Store character furnishes the choice

Below, the plain background; *immediate right*, two examples of the decorated background. Snaith says, "Presentation, setting, background lend value and glamour to stock; enhance it, interpret its taste level, say something positive about it. Decoration has proved to be the best possible way to stimulate sales of all kinds of merchandise . . . whether or not the goods themselves have high fashion appeal."

INSIDE TIPS

1. Never put a fur department near a stairway or escalator or entrance. The annual loss from stolen goods is calculated and estimated and entered as a cost of operation.

2. Place impulse items at the foot of "down" electric stairs. With his purchase completed upstairs, the captive customer's vision is now forced downward, and she is liable to buy impulse merchandise on the way *out*.

3. A restaurant is almost mandatory in a branch store. In suburban communities stores virtually empty out at lunch time. If you don't feed a customer on the premises you lose her for the day. She'll get into the bad habit of shopping around the neighborhood for the balance of the afternoon.

4. Men are not repelled by a "feminine" color scheme in a store: in branch stores men shop with women; downtown, they shop alone.

5. Beauty parlors in branch stores usually are not very profitable. The amount of revenue produced by the beauty shop is less than the revenue produced by using the space for other purposes. They take up too much space in a situation where space is limited.

EXTERIOR CHARACTER

In wrapping a building around the plan, we must consider esthetics, of course, but we must also be ruled by budget and cost of maintenance. A store is the most commercial of commercial buildings, and building cost appears as "cost of operation" under the heading "occupancy." Maintenance cost appears in the same column of the same ledger.

There are implied operational hazards in certain treatments. Unfortunately, the glass wall is an enemy of merchandising. It is virtually impossible to display against it—light cannot be controlled. The glass wall imposes a costly maintenance factor, for the outside view changes constantly according to what is happening inside. Yet we like glass areas, and therefore use them where they penalize us least. Daylight does accent interior lighting; breaks the monotony of masonry expanses. For these reasons, certain departments can be located to provide an interesting façade. The glass wall is appropriate for restaurant, employe, and office areas. Only two types of sales operations can live under glass: those wherein the merchandise itself has decorative value, as gifts; or those not requiring exposed stock, as a salon, which sells only by atmosphere and total image.

The exterior should project several images: 1, size (because the department store should say, visually, it is the strongest purveyor of goods in the area); 2, permanence and institutionality (to instill a sense of trust and dependability); 3, definition from its neighbors (restrained if nearby buildings are flashy, etc.); 4, the nature of merchandise and customer (where one finds ideas, stimulation, taste); 5, store character (high fashion, graceful, fine in scale—institutional, solid, no nonsense); 6, regional or community character. Unless the store reflects the community, it may never get built. Exterior character as much as store reputation will make a design acceptable locally.

INTERIOR CHARACTER

When we come to interior treatment, we emphasize —by every device—the projection of the total store image. That character or image, as we have seen, is a composite of the store's merchandise, its way of doing business, its customer, its position in relation to all other merchants handling like merchandise.

Inside the store the projection of this image is accomplished through display. "Display" in this sense has the broad meaning of showing merchandise against controlled backgrounds that enhance and facilitate selling—not narrowed to mean the art of dressing windows, draping apparel on mannequins, or arranging counter top eye-catchers.

FIXTURES are the basis of display, and their location, type, and design establishes character and enables the store to operate within its own peculiar method of merchandising.

Labor is a store's most expensive commodity; retailing has been described as the last of the manual industries. If we plan fixtures to reduce the amount of sales help we save in operation cost, but this reduction automatically lowers the level of presentation. In fixture design we must seek some comfortable median between turning the store into a supermarket (maximum self-selection and self-service) and a salon where the customer is individually helped at every stage of the sale. Personnel cost pushes up merchandise price, and there is a point somewhere here of no return.

In general, a floor comprises three major sections; a central section of islands and aisles, plus two sides. Smallwares or impulse items are in the central section, in which open fixtures—counter height—are combined to make islands. The sides carry merchandise requiring wall fixtures. Since our plan example is based on a peripheral stock arrangement, these departments back up into stock. We have now a picture of a store wherein the first impression is of highly visible impulse items, a long and wide general view of full stock, and inviting glimpses around the periphery of the floor of entrances to shops having individual, appropriate character.

DECORATION. Fifteen years ago, many merchants resisted the idea of a decorated, dramatically interpreted background for goods. They felt a background assertive enough to give a positive impression of fashion would overpower the merchandise. On the contrary, it has proved to be the best possible way to stimulate sales of all kinds of merchandise; and this is true whether or not the goods have high fashion appeal. Merchandise itself, item by item, is difficult to evaluate. Even expert buyers find it virtually impossible to distinguish between two unknown items (with tags removed) priced at 7.95 and 12.95!

Presentation, setting, background lend value and glamour to stock; enhance it, interpret its taste lev-

The electric stairway as a major dramatic feature. In Gimbel's Valley Stream branch, marble, glass, and special lighting are used to that end. Note the illuminated store directory

el, say something positive about it. Today, "fashion" is the most potent incentive to buy, and in a branch store fashion is the impression desired. Background can also say that merchandise is of unassailable quality, or is a good bargain, or that it's the newest. Skirts in a sportswear department are hung together—12 to the foot—and differences cannot be detected. Therefore, surroundings, fixtures, and decoration must create a feeling of quality that reassures the customer that anything in the department must be good.

Graphics can establish character directly and at little cost. Upper wall areas, valances, counter or rack ends, all provide surfaces for such treatments. Color is one of the most consciously registered indications of style, and can be introduced in graphic variations. Stained woods in color, synthetics, fabrics, paint, plaster, mirror—all can serve to introduce both color and textural change of pace.

CEILING HEIGHTS are of course determined by the size of the visible space; the larger the space the higher the ceiling—within reason. But since we want a maximum of flexibility, fixtures form interior walls. They often do not reach the ceiling, so we can save building cost by using a lower ceiling than the total space would seem to indicate. Upper air space use is affected by the optical necessities of signs, and by devices indicating shop groupings. Case top screens and dividers can indicate areas and provide additional space for decoration.

Attempts to create a sense of height by varying ceiling levels may be imperative in modernization work, but in new buildings are inadvisable. When ceilings are dropped, flexibility suffers.

LIGHTING is an indispensable tool of modern merchandising. Without up-to-date lighting and air conditioning, there could be no peripheral plan. Fluorescent lighting alone tends to flatten out merchandise and render it in monotonous sameness. Therefore use fluorescent to provide an overall light level, and then add the expensive, heat producing—but irreplaceable—incandescent light for visual kicks. A grid pattern that can be varied endlessly characterizes the store ceiling—which incorporates lighting, air-conditioning outlets, and sprinklers. Sometimes the grid is a reflected pattern of the plan below; often it is merely a pleasing geometric pattern.

ELECTRIC STAIRWAYS handle vertical traffic best, and their treatment is an important design consideration. Since they cannot be construed as a merchandising device, they should be handled as a major decorative and dramatic feature. This can be accomplished by means of architectural excitement, color, expensive materials, lighting, etc. The result should have a "look" of permanence, not intransigence.

THE SMALL SHOP

Many principles of branch store design apply to small shop assignments. Since space is limited and so is merchandise, space allocation is enormously simplified. In small shop design it is important to follow the rule of using the exterior to make the impact of store character on the customer; and to make the interior give the best possible impression of the capacity of that shop to contain, display, and sell merchandise. This calls for a shift in approach from exterior to interior. In the branch store this is done *within the store* in handling individual departments where the impact is made at the entrance to a shop or department, not through a window.

Thus, in designing the small shop exterior, adapt the merchandise *display* to the outside; adapt the interior plan and design to *merchandising* needs.

The total image of fashion store; J. W. Robinson, Beverly Hills, Cal.,

Bake Shop—Wall Painting from Pompeii

SHOPS AND THE MARKET PLACE

by Morris Ketchum, Jr.

11

1

2

3

The sole function of a shop is to sell. Every shop or store is therefore a basically simple planning problem. It consists in a sales area where goods are displayed and sold (1), a service area for handling incoming and outgoing merchandise, and a store front used to advertise the business within.

These three elements must be planned to suit the sales and operating methods of the retailer, the buying habits of his customers, and the shopping environment in which the shop is placed.

Store planning has followed this formula since the dawn of history.

The heart of any retail establishment is the space where merchant and customer meet over the sales counter. A sales area that is well organized for over-the-counter operations can be compared to an indoor shopping street. Its various merchandise departments should be arranged on the customer traffic aisles like shops along an outdoor thoroughfare (2). These departments are best located in a horizontal or vertical (3) sequence, starting at the entrance door, of *impulse, convenience* and *demand* goods.

The merchandise on sale in a shop or store will be largely demand in character with a generous assortment of impulse and convenience items added to complete the picture. The economic success of any shop depends on how well it stimulates impulse buying. The purchase of household furniture is a demand transaction; the purchase of living room bric-a-brac an impulse sale that may make the difference between a day's profit or loss.

The store planner's first job is to locate and interrelate all types of merchandise for maximum impulse buying and to take full advantage of every square foot of sales area for selling functions. After that, he must tie the selling space to its own non-selling areas, to the store front and to the outdoor shopping environment.

Page 12

Ever since peddlers settled down to fixed locations in some market place and started to deal with sidewalk traffic, shopping environment has played a vital part in the design of shops and stores. From then on, store fronts have been built to provide, in varied ways, on-the-spot contact between the customers out front and the merchant inside. Their design has expressed the different ways of living, trading and building in successive civilizations, but the basic solution has always been the same. The shops of ancient Rome, of medieval Europe, or of Colonial days are strikingly similar to those today in all except technical detail.

The market place changes more often than its shops and stores.

City and suburban market places were first organized for foot traffic only (4). Over-the-sidewalk displays and advertising, store fronts and signs, were in direct contact with the shopping crowd. Then horse drawn, and finally, motor driven traffic, broke into the picture and destroyed ideal contact between merchant and consumer. The market place became hazardous environment for customers and a less profitable one for merchants. It became more and more difficult to do business in a traffic jam.

During the nineteenth century and the first half of the twentieth, our shopping districts lost all resemblance to older and quieter market places (5). Except within the special indoor environment provided by our giant department stores, shopping became a dangerous obstacle race. Downtown shopping conditions were essentially the same in our towns, cities and suburbs from coast to coast (6). The street pattern inherited from horse and buggy days had become overcrowded and unsafe. Private automobiles had no place to park, busses collected and left their passengers at random street corners, trucks had only curbside unloading terminals. Noise, confusion and congestion made life irritating for both shopper and motorist.

4

5

6

Florsheim Shoes

7

ALBERT McGANN
SECURITIES

8

In spite of all this, downtown shop fronts are still designed for pedestrians because no one can park and shop from an automobile window. They attempt to catch the distant eye with overhead signs that can be seen across the street above the intervening stream of motor traffic (7). These shops fronts are sometimes visually closed and directly on the building line, especially for service establishments with no goods to display (8). More often, the trend is towards a front that is set back from the building line in order to enlarge the sidewalk and to create display in depth (9). With more elbow room and quieter conditions, window shoppers can spend more time inspecting show windows and the interior sales floor. Fully glazed store fronts and entrance doors (10) help to eliminate any visual barriers between the moving crowd on the sidewalk and sales area inside. Today's shop fronts are cleverly designed picture frames for merchandising stage sets (11).

9

10

11

12

13

Even the best shops and stores cannot win against the wrong shopping environment. During the last ten years, the danger point has been reached—in New York alone, eight major department stores closed their doors forever. Merchants and their architects have tried to regain traffic-free outdoor space for shoppers and to provide off-street parking and trucking in one form or another, all in an effort to meet suburban competition. Pedestrian plazas set within building sites (12-13-14) have partially enlarged the city's sidewalks, freed buildings from their neighbors and increased the amenities of downtown life. Today, there is a great surge of urban redevelopment projects. In city after city—Pittsburgh, Boston, Chicago, New York, Denver—attempts are being made to redevelop and reestablish the central shopping district.

14

16

15

Partial redevelopment is not enough—entire downtown areas must be remodeled if the growth of decentralized shopping is to be balanced by an upturn in urban shopping volume. Down in Texas, where people like to think and act on a big scale, Fort Worth has put the redemption of its central business district ahead of any other civic improvement. It is determined to cope with the blight, congestion, and shopping paralysis that threaten its existence.

Fort Worth has a compact city core of more than 300 acres bounded by a river and railroad lines (15). This core will be encircled with a belt highway. On the inner side of this belt highway a series of giant parking garages will be located. Incoming and outgoing motorists will never penetrate the heart of the city. City busses will take the belt highway around the business district. Below street level, truck deliveries will be made from the belt highway by means of a tunnel loop servicing every city block. Beyond the central core, the new belt highway will be fed by existing arterial highways. Motor traffic will be organized, *tamed* and given proper terminals.

The mile square heart of Fort Worth then becomes a pedestrian paradise (16). Each street will be a sidewalk. Planting islands, covered walkways, kiosks, little shops, frequent areas for rest and recreation, trees and fountains, turn the whole business district into a public park. For the weary, laden, infirm and lazy, there will be small electric busses, similar to those used at world's fairs, to carry them from shop to shop, or from office to lunch, or the theatre.

The Fort Worth plan has its economic advantages as well. City maintenance costs will be reduced, city land will be regained and sold to private developers, business and shopping will prosper and yield more municipal taxes. The entire project should be self-liquidating.

The importance of the Fort Worth plan is that it points the way towards the regeneration of downtown urban areas from coast to coast. No plan of this type can be realized overnight, but each stage of progressive rebuilding will help to revitalize a central shopping district.

18

17

19

Department stores have always had—indoors—the controlled shopping environment that our urban centers are striving to regain. These retailing giants are equivalent in scope and size to a multitude of specialty shops all located under one roof and under one management. As such, they can be in themselves an indoor shopping center.

A quarter century ago, most department stores looked like warehouses. Their gridiron traffic aisles resembled the gridiron streets of the outdoor city. Their customers became footsore and bewildered by monotonous acres of merchandise. Today, some department stores may still look like warehouses but most of them have been reorganized as indoor shopping centers where every sales department is designed as a separate shop, and carefully located in good relationship to its neighbors and to freely planned traffic aisles. Sales departments compete with sales departments in style and price, so that customers may enjoy all the benefits of comparative shopping just as they do along some outdoor Main Street. The shopping environment—lighting and climate, displays and sales backgrounds, atmosphere and character—is a tightly controlled indoor version of an outdoor shopping center.

Department stores are also beginning to solve for themselves the traffic and parking problems of a downtown shopping environment.

In the Court House Square Development set in the heart of Denver, Colorado, two city blocks have been rebuilt as an integrated urban development consisting of the May D & F department store, a 900-room hotel, a lower level shopping center, and an underground parking garage (17). The department store is linked with the main shopping street by a unique entrance pavilion which is, in itself, a giant showcase containing women's accessories shops. A covered bridge links the fashion floor of the department store and the hotel restaurant at second floor level. Customers are brought up by elevator from the garage below. The lower level shopping center is in direct contact with the basement store of the department store. Finally, the winter time skating rink becomes an outdoor promotion area for the department store in the summer months. The entire development thus has all the advantages and all the glamour of a suburban shopping center, yet is located in the heart of downtown Denver.

A perfume shop and gourmet food shop shed their store fronts and take their place on customer aisles within urban department stores. The perfume shop (18) is small in size and lightly organized. Its merchandise is stocked by brand name in separate sales fixtures; its background wall identifies the shop and conceals a reserve stock area. The gourmet shop (19) is identified by an illuminated mural wall of translucent glass. Its goods are stocked and displayed on metal-framed floor fixtures and wall shelving. The alcove location helps to establish its shop-like atmosphere.

20

21

22

These two sales divisions within department stores have all the intimate atmosphere of specialty shops. Special ceilings (20) or display walls (21) mark their boundaries. Lighting, color schemes, materials, textures, character, are powerfully organized to attract customers wandering down the indoor shopping street. Departments of this kind must compete against other sales divisions featuring similar merchandise differently priced or styled. Both departments are in suburban Baltimore stores, both cater to women, both are well organized.

One of the current trends in shop design is an increasing emphasis on decorative character, expressed in murals, lighting fixtures, signs, furniture and displays. This children's shoe shop in a branch department store (22) sums up the casual informality so often associated with suburban shopping.

Department store buildings, too, reflect the character of this shopping environment. As compared with downtown stores, informality and local character are the architectural keynotes, used to express a casual country atmosphere without any loss of institutional prestige. Shown is a sketch of such a branch department store (23) organized on three shopping levels and set on a sloping site that permits entrances at two of these three levels. Its largely windowless exterior is saved from monotony by a pattern of brick panels in alternate colors, set flush or recessed, which expresses in a decorative way the sales floors within the building.

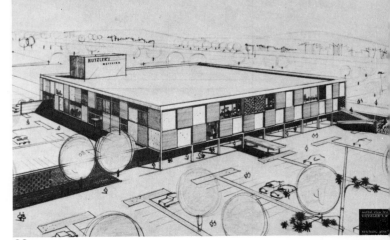

23

GARDEN COURT

24   25

The controlled indoor shopping environment of a typical department store has influenced the design of a prototype shopping center. In this project, two department stores and a multitude of small shops are clustered on two levels around an enclosed two-story, air conditioned, indoor shopping concourse enlivened with trees, planting beds, pools, statuary, garden courts, and recreational areas (24). The shops themselves sometimes have open entrances (25); sometimes, more conventional glazed store fronts (26). Like department store sales divisions, they are properly related to each other and to the overall customer traffic pattern.

26

27

During World War II, the first suburban shopping center with a pedestrian mall, a ring of shops and stores and an outer ring of parking was built near San Diego. Linda Vista (*27*) established a new building type and started a revolution in shopping environment. Since then, giant regional shopping centers have been planned and built all over the country. These centers have solved the interrelated problems of auto traffic, parking facilities, truck traffic, pedestrian traffic and the specialized planning problems of large groups of stores.

Store locations are worked out along their shopping concourses so as to group related shops by trade classifications, to spot powerful traffic generators such as department stores in key locations, to en-

courage comparison shopping and to maintain an even flow of traffic throughout the entire center.

All shops and stores are in direct contact with foot traffic on the pleasant covered walkways, landscaped plazas and outdoor shopping areas. Shopping hazards and design handicaps created by motor traffic are kept away from this new green world where shopping has gained the pleasant environment of a garden and the gaiety of a carnival.

These new opportunities are accompanied by a new restriction—the necessity for overall harmony of design. Shop interiors and shop fronts must be kept within bounds set by uniform roof heights and arcade dimensions. Signs and color schemes are regulated and restrained for the common good. Only

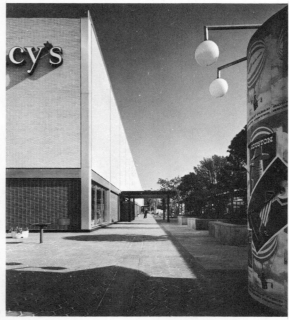

30

31

28

29

big department store units and other special buildings can escape such overall rules and regulations.

Shown are two shopping centers where these rules have been applied along outdoor shopping concourses. In the first one (*28*), the rules for signs have been formulated along lines similar to those used downtown. The signs above the canopy are far above pedestrian eye-level and are still trying to assert themselves over and above an imaginary stream of motor traffic. In the second (*29*), the signs are more successful. They are located below the canopy at the proper eye-level and are controlled by the design of the canopy and the sign areas themselves.

One of the most pleasant and sophisticated shopping environments ever produced exists in the

Roosevelt Field Shopping Center. Its architectural detail (*30-31-32*), landscape design (*31*), fountains (*32*), flags and street furniture are all outstanding. These, added to all the usual advantages of a well planned regional center, make it a pleasant place for shoppers and a profitable site for shops.

Many of these shops are located where they can draw on two streams of customer traffic. On one side, their principal entrance taps the traffic stream of one of the main shopping arcades (*32*); on the other side, a minor entrance faces one of the exterior customer parking areas. On the following pages, one of these shops is presented as an example of how such a location and shopping environment affect the organization of a small shop in a suburban center.

32

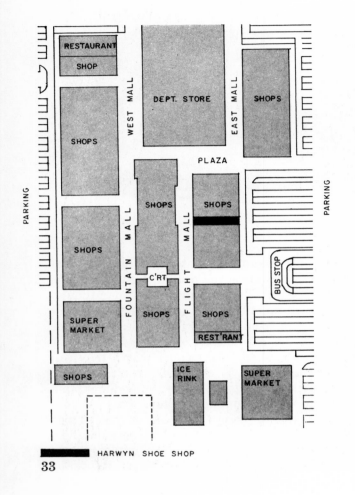

HARWYN SHOE SHOP

33

The Harwyn Shoes Store at Roosevelt Field Shopping Center [*33*] is a small shop that is treated like a miniature department store. It sells men's shoes, women's accessories, women's shoes, and children's shoes. Its plan [*34*] and interior design express this merchandising program. There are separate but interlocking sales departments, each with its own distinctive character, arranged in the above sequence from the mall entrance [*35*] to the parking area entrance [*36*]. These successive sales units help to break up a narrow, corridor-like sales area into a series of well proportioned spaces.

The garden mall entrance [*35*] is a display lobby with depth enough to feature all types of merchandise sold. Women's shoes occupy the island show window; men's shoes the full height windows at the left; women's shoes and accessories are shown in the shadow boxes at the right; children's shoes in the right rear show window. Both fluorescent and incandescent light sources add sparkle to the lobby and its displays.

LOBBY   MEN'S DEPARTMENT   WOMEN'S DEPARTMENT

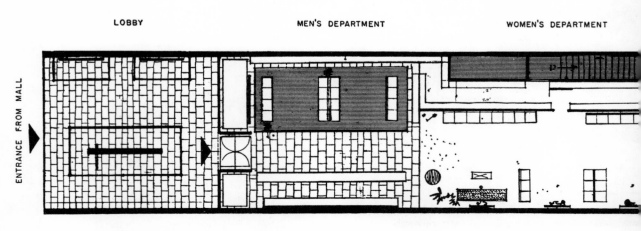

ACCESSORIES

35

CHILDREN'S DEPARTMENT

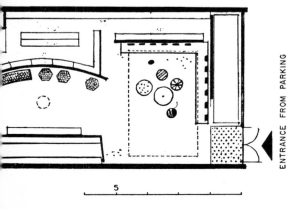

ENTRANCE FROM PARKING

5

36

Men's shoes (*37*) are stocked along the rear wall of that department. The yellow color of the stock boxes is reflected in a gold toned carpet. A natural teak fin wall, a hung ceiling in light gray, and another low fin wall display bound the department within its alcove. Opposite, metal-framed counters and wall fixtures, backed by a large display panel, set the stage for women's handbags, costume jewelry and miscellaneous accessories (*38*).

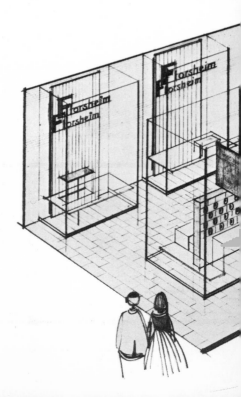

38

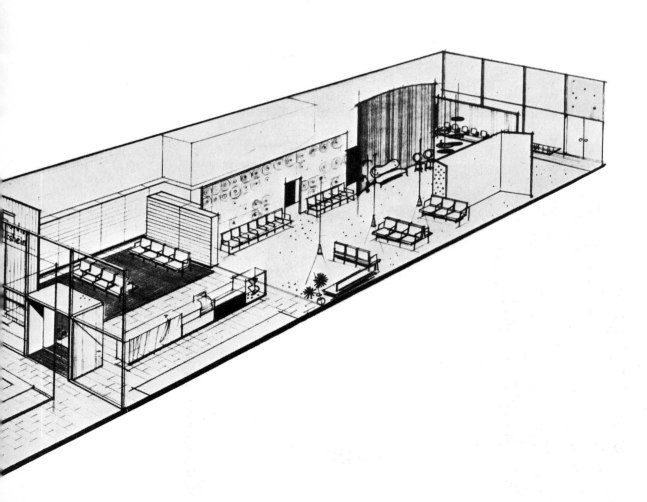

39

41

28

40

The pink painted wall of reeded wood travels behind this panel and on into the women's budget shoe department (*39*), which is followed by a special section for higher priced women's shoes (*40*). Here one wall is curtained in a black fabric shot with blue, the other wallpapered in gray and white. The curtained wall conceals a reserve stock area.

At the end of the store is the children's shoe department (*41*). Another hung ceiling in deep maroon, walls in light gray, and child size furniture in gay upholstery colors set the tone of this area. The circular ceiling pattern ties in with a nursery toy display platforms. This department is visible to customers entering from the adjacent parking area (*42*). At night, the illuminated name sign gives effective identification across the parking area.

42

LIST OF ILLUSTRATIONS, PAGES 12 TO 30

PHOTO CREDITS

43

SHOP DESIGNED LIKE A DISPLAY CASE

Textiles & Objects Shop
A Division of Herman Miller, Inc.
New York, N. Y.
ARCHITECT: *Alexander Girard*

The primary effect of this shop is that of a life-size showcase, through which the customer may pass to view the fabrics designed by Alexander Girard and the folk art selected by him. For both the retail and wholesale trade, the showcase presents its wares in an atmosphere of gayety and liveliness. The interior is revealed to passers-by on the street through the store-wide, ceiling-high glass front. The narrow, deep interior space—20 by 100 ft—is modulated by hanging fabric display panels that form overlapping vertical planes, which partially reveal, partially conceal the displays. The background, against which the colorful textiles and folk art objects are shown—the walls, floors, and ceilings—is white and strictly neutral. The ceiling sparkles with 350 silvered, reflector light bulbs set in strips parallel to the street and 36 in. on centers. Flexible display fixtures include a special picture molding and ceiling strips for hanging fabrics and display towers that support shelves and contain lighting.

Todd Webb photos

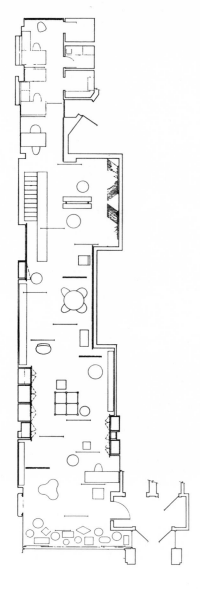

As indicated in the plan, the interior space of this shop is narrow and quite deep. The architect subdivided and defined this long space by hanging fabrics from the ceiling, at the same time achieving proper display for the fabrics themselves. The furniture, all manufactured by the shop owner, is used sparingly to create a homelike atmosphere and, at the same time, provide a method for display of some of the folk art objects. Other objects are placed on display towers shown in the illustration at top of page

UNDULATING PLYWOOD ATTRACTS CUSTOMERS

Pine Lumber Company Showroom
Detroit, Michigan
ARCHITECTS: *Hawthorne & Schmiedeke*

By using plywood, one of the materials sold in this building, in an exciting and imaginative manner, the architects of this showroom have caused the building itself to act as a most effective advertisement for the products displayed within. The unusual, undulating roof, which seems to float airily over the structure, is constructed of 3-ft 3-in. deep plywood girders, on 11-ft 8-in. centers, with top and bottom skins each fabricated from two layers of quarter inch fir plywood. Girders have four by ten top and bottom chords. Plywood skins are stapled and glued together and similarly fastened to girders and to two by fours laid flat at center points between girders. Four by eight columns are framed into the roof system at ends of girders. The interior of the roof system is painted; its joints are covered by redwood battens and continuous fluorescent light fixtures. Roofing is built-up composition with marble chips; fascias are scored sheet metal.

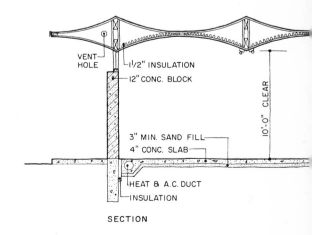

VENT HOLE
1½" INSULATION
12" CONC. BLOCK
3" MIN. SAND FILL
4" CONC. SLAB
10'-0" CLEAR
HEAT & A.C. DUCT
INSULATION

SECTION

Pine Lumber Company Showroom

Baltazar Korab ©

The large—56 by 117 ft—plywood roof protects the interior which primarily consists of about two-thirds display area and sales counter space and one-third office area. In addition to its obvious value as an attention-getter, the roof frees the floor area for more flexible use for display of the company's products, which are stored in the lumber yard behind the building.

Other than the roof, the building is constructed of conventional materials. The flooring is terrazzo over a concrete slab. Walls are patterned concrete block and glass. Windows are redwood, with painted solid panels under fixed glass

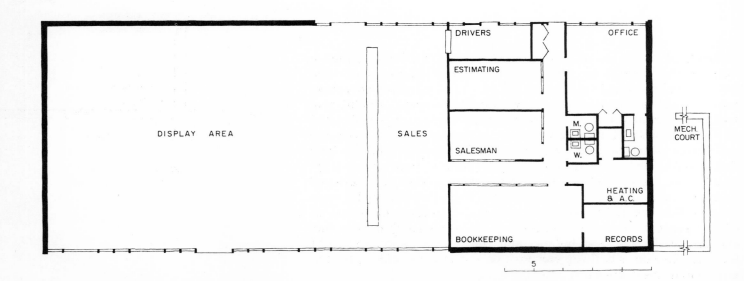

TO MAKE A SMALL STORE LOOK LARGER

F. J. Cooper Store, Philadelphia
ARCHITECTS: *Geddes-Brecher-Qualls & Cunningham*
STRUCTURAL ENGINEER: *David Bloom*
MECHANICAL ENGINEERS: *Cronheim & Weger*
CONTRACTOR: *John P. Hallahan*

Regarding the design of this elegant little jewelry shop in down-town Philadelphia, architect George W. Qualls says, "Many shops of small area have a cluttered look about them that reduces their effectiveness as a display vehicle. For this store, most design decisions were determined by the need to produce a sense of spaciousness and the desire to make the objects on display the main focal points of the interior. The plaster vaulting, calculated to make walls and ceiling flow together, was used to bring the eye down to the wall cases. Similarly, the gray carpeting was carried up the wall behind the cases in order to destroy the junctures of wall with floor and provide a neutral backdrop for the wall displays. Because of the flowing linear quality of these elements, the space manages to achieve an air of expansiveness it might have lost if the scheme were entirely rectilinear. The exterior arches are a direct expression of the two interior vaults immediately inside; one arch is the entrance, the other a recessed window display."

© 1962 F. W. Dodge Corporation

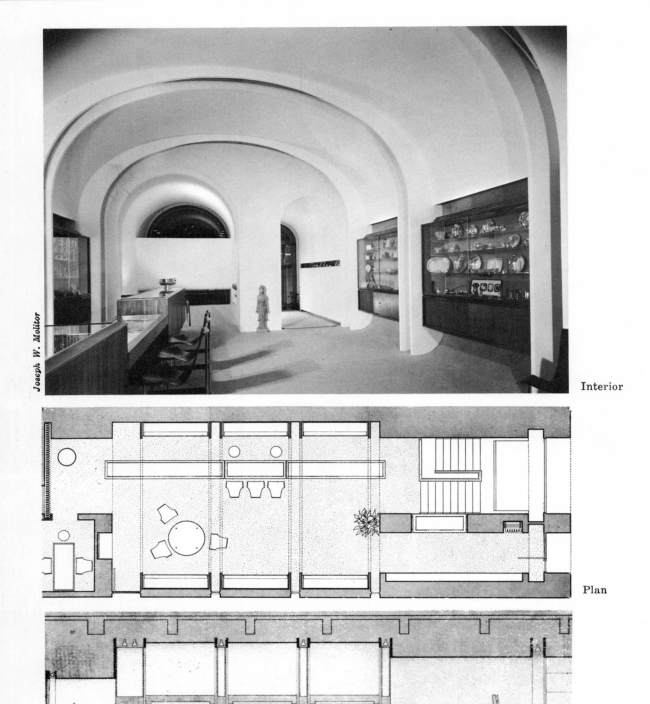

Joseph W. Molitor

Interior

Plan

Section

The variety of the materials used in the store was consciously held to a minimum. Basically, there are white plaster ribs and vaults—constructed with furring channels and metal lath—walnut casework, and gray carpeting. Bronze sash and trim, plus yellow and gray curtains for contrast

CAMPUS BOOKSTORE AND POST OFFICE

Stanford University, Palo Alto, California

ARCHITECT: *John Carl Warnecke & Associates*

STRUCTURAL ENGINEER: *Isadore Thompson*

MECHANICAL ENGINEER: *Kasin, Guttman and Malayan*

LANDSCAPE ARCHITECT: *Thomas D. Church*

GENERAL CONTRACTOR: *Howard J. White*

The new Book Store and Post Office for Stanford University—second phase of a building program which will eventually provide a nine-building student activity center—contribute significantly to the development of a new expression of the University's architectural tradition. For these two buildings, with their graceful, flat-arched arcades and buff-colored concrete, respectfully acknowledge the strong statement of the early "Quad" buildings (by Shepley, Rutan and Coolidge) and the rusticated buff stone, red tile roofs and many arches which are the campus hallmark; but they do this in their own completely contemporary idiom. Materials and technique as much as design make possible this new approach. Built at a cost of $489,569, the Book Store's main sales area is a clear space 65 by 85 ft, with a 100-ft skylight above; on the balcony are more display shelves (in all, 400 books can be displayed), and offices.

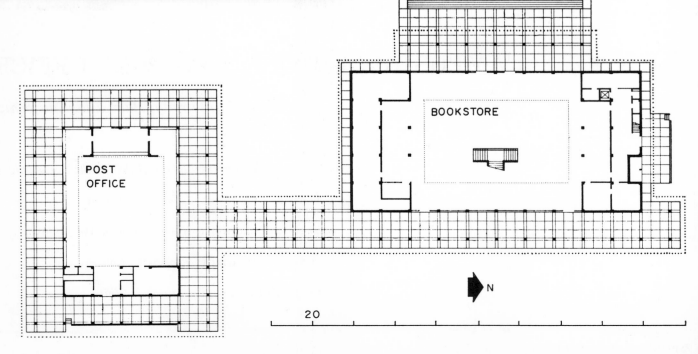

POST OFFICE

BOOKSTORE

N

20

The vaulted forms were precast and lifted into place on top of the cast-in-place columns; joints were then grouted. Concrete bents for roof and wall framing were also precast; after placing of the vaults, these were hoisted to positions 15 ft o.c. Their loads are transmitted to columns through connections at column tops. The system frees walls for a variety of fillers: concrete block with stucco finish for solid walls; large glass panels on both sides of the Book Store for light and transparency in the sales space; and two-way mail boxes in the Post Office which save interior floor space and give sparkle to exterior walls

Book store interior (top) keeps the feeling of a single great space, lofty, light and spacious, while accommodating very extensive book stocks in open displays all accessible to customers (or browsers)

JOHN & EDWARD BUMPUS, LTD., LONDON W1

David Rock, Architect

J. Musgrove & N. Watson, Lighting Consultants

NEW BOOKSHOP FOR OLD LONDON BOOKSELLERS

Alfred Cracknell photos

In this small London bookshop, the architect has managed a relaxed contemporary atmosphere which is accepted and appreciated by the owners and customers alike. This is quite an accomplishment in Baker Street. It seems even more of an accomplishment when one considers that the architect's clients were the oldest booksellers in London (the firm was founded in 1790), and hold the Royal Warrant.

The shop occupies two ground floor bays and the basement of an eight-story building. Provisions are made for customers to browse, or sit and read in comfort. The view from the street is inviting and congenial. The interior is restrained, but possessed of great warmth, extremely comfortable, but spare.

© 1959 F. W. Dodge Corporation

Of his design, the architect says, "A bookstore is somewhat of a cross between a library and a self-service store. Therefore, I tried to create a congenial background for leisurely shopping. Further, my purpose was to surround the occupants with a space which was unobtrusive, yet one which would also be recognizable as architecture." In order to achieve these purposes, the shop has been designed with restrained good taste, as is evident in the illustrations. The rich materials such as marble, African walnut, copper, and leather contrast with simple white plastered walls. Sculpture is placed in a number of locations, in an attempt to integrate this art with those of literature and architecture

WASHINGTON AIRCRAFT AND TRANSPORT CORP.,
SEATTLE, WASH.

Mithun, Ridenour and Cochran, Architects
Gerard Torrence, Structural Engineer
Puget Construction Co., Contractor

AIRPORT SALES OFFICE FOR PRIVATE PLANES

Art Hupy photos

At this location, the sales and servicing of small private aircraft are separated from those related activities involved in sales and storage of parts, office functions, and the like. In order to accomplish this to the best possible advantage, the architects designed two closely related buildings, a hangar for the airplanes and an office building for the other functions.

Both buildings were designed for economical construction, ease of maintenance, and efficient operation. The buildings are comfortable and provide the atmosphere the clients desired for their customers and company personnel. The structure is quite simple, the materials clean and unobtrusive, in harmony with the location and purpose of the buildings.

© 1959 F. W. Dodge Corporation

43

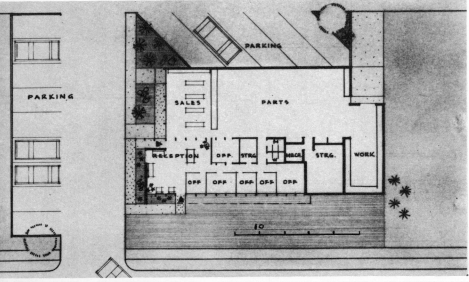

The extreme simplicity of the office building is indicated in the plan shown above. This feeling is reflected in the interior. The structure and materials used are not extraordinary—exposed concrete bearing walls and bar joists, with a wood-fiber cement board roof. Thus, the materials serve not only as structure, but also double as finishes. Additionally, the roof deck acts as insulation and acoustical treatment. The resulting economy has not obviated good appearance. The hangar building, shown below, is constructed with a clear-span rigid steel frame, for the utmost in flexibility of the space. Concrete block walls are used for enclosure only, and one wall is composed entirely of sliding doors for maximum utility

DEXTER CHEVROLET, INC., DETROIT, MICH.

King & Lewis, Architects

R. H. McClurg & Assoc., Structural Engineers

Migdal & Layne, Mechanical & Electrical Engineers

Henry Slatkin Builders, Contractors

AN EFFECTIVE BACKGROUND FOR AUTO SALES

Baltazar Korab ©

The architects of this building wished to express something of the assembly line, machine product qualities of the automobiles it will house. However, it was felt that the building must serve as background for the products, not compete with them in any way. This, with the added desire for architectural excitement, was the goal set for the design.

In order to accomplish their aims, the architects have provided for complete sales and service functions within a plain, rectangular building and added to this an exciting showroom on the front. This wing with its vaulted roof and floor to ceiling glass contrasts mightily with the austerity of the remainder of the building. The result fulfills the functions programmed.

Dexter Chevrolet

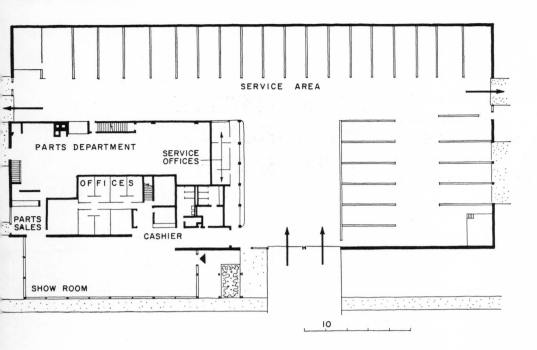

Ballazar Korab ©

 As may be seen in the plan, the relationships between the pedestrian entrance, showrooms, offices, parts sales and storage, and service areas have been worked out for a smooth flow of operations. The automobile entrance and exits make the movement of cars through the various phases of service as easy as possible, with very little congestion. The illustrations indicate some of the clean qualities of the structure and materials used. These include steel frame and concrete vaults, concrete block and face brick, with blue, white, and gray porcelain enamel panels at the entrance, and terrazzo floors. Wood paneling set in light steel office partition framing is used for division of interior spaces wherever feasible

UNUSUAL TWO-LEVEL
SERVICING ARRANGEMENT

The May Company
University Heights, Ohio

The May Company

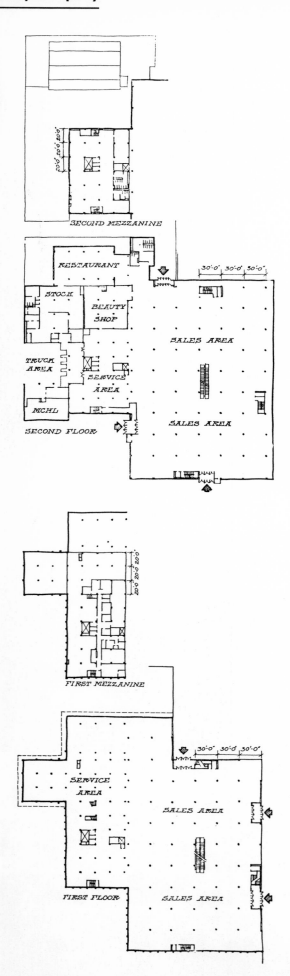

SECOND MEZZANINE

RESTAURANT

STOCK

BEAUTY SHOP

SALES AREA

TRUCK AREA

SERVICE AREA

MCHL

SECOND FLOOR

SALES AREA

30'-0" 30'-0" 30'-0"

FIRST MEZZANINE

SERVICE AREA

SALES AREA

FIRST FLOOR

SALES AREA

The May Company, University Heights, Ohio. Victor Gruen Associates, Architects; Jack Alan Bialosky, Associate Architect; Sam W. Emerson Company, General Contractors; Swanson Associates, Sales Area Interiors.

A separated service tower, containing two floors to every one in the sales area, is the operational and architectural feature of this branch store. It is a modification of the central service core idea that was used in Northland. But here, in a store with a considerably smaller floor area, it was felt that the central core would create too much of a visual barrier in the retailing space; hence it was moved to one end of the rectangular sales block.

Within the tower itself, the floors aligning with the sales floors are used for direct servicing and goods handling, while intermediate floors are used for storage or non-selling activities such as alteration and busheling rooms, employes' restaurant, lounge, offices, etc. Air handling equipment is also located on the in-between levels, making possible a great deal of flexibility in the development of the air conditioning system. Boilers and compressors are in a penthouse, freeing additional tower space for essential store functions.

To reduce the floor-to-floor heights in the sales block, that unit was developed as a flat slab structure with columns at 30 ft on centers; while the service tower was developed in steel frame—with minimum column spacing—in order to cut the tower floor heights to an absolute minimum.

The site had a natural elevation differential of 25 ft from a V-shaped lower area near the highway intersection to the rear. The building is placed well back on the plot so the lower level is served by an extensive parking area, which in turn is surmounted on three sides by higher-level parking for the upper floor. The actual result is a store with two first floors, plus great flexibility in developing traffic flow.

All photos by Jack Sterling

Due to the scarcity of high class dining places in the area, the restaurant—designed by architect Gruen—was given special consideration. It was developed as a semi-independent structure adjacent to a garden within a high wall. which contains as its visual focus a year-around decorative fountain designed by Richard H. Jennings.

By separating the restaurant structure and giving it independent entrance, it became feasible to operate it on a schedule different from the normal store pattern. This means that the owners can—if they wish—develop a seven-days-a-week dinner business

AN ARCHITECTURE FOR DAY AND NIGHT

De Bijenkorf Department Store
Rotterdam

ARCHITECTS: *Marcel Breuer and A. Elzas*

CONSULTANT: *Daniel Schwartzman*

SCULPTURER: *Naum Gabo*

THIS DESIGN OFFERS an intriguing answer to the architectural problem of how to sheathe the upper merchandising floors of a department store. Here, a fenestration pattern that interestingly and dramatically reverses itself from daylight to dark is set within a striated travertine curtain in hexagonal pattern. The glazed slits not only rob the wall of its nudity, but also give the customer the traditional prerogative of examining his purchase by natural light (important in Holland) without destroying the usefulness of the entire wall space for merchandising or storage.

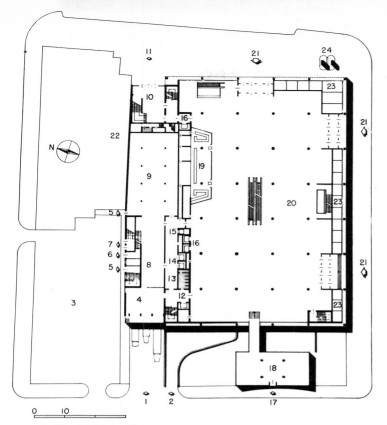

GROUND FLOOR PLAN

1. Deliveries	9. Marking	17. Pavilion Entrance
2. Underground Garage	10. Cineac Lobby	18. Pavilion
3. Parking	11. Cineac Entrance	19. Snack Bar
4. Receiving	12. Elevator—Personnel	20. Sales Area
5. Personnel Entrance	13. Personnel	21. Public Entrance
6. Public Entrance	14. Elevator—Freight	22. Hotel Atlanta
7. Cinema Exit	15. Elevator—Kitchen	23. Show Windows
8. Packaging	16. Elevator—Public	24. Sculpture

The 82 ft. metal sculpture by Naum Gabo serves as projection at the corner, required by the plan for rebuilding the 650 acres of downtown Rotterdam destroyed in the 1940 air attack. The Cineac movie theater is faced in black brick and set back from the main facade line to form a small plaza.

The twin motor entrances, shown left and bottom, lead to the loading dock and to basement parking.

Photos on pages 52, 53, and top of 51 by Frits Monshouwer; bottom of page 51 by Robert Doisneau

The solidity of the main parallelepiped — clad in travertine and resting on a base of gray granite — is nicely countered not alone by the fenestration pattern but also by the weblike, refined curtain wall enclosing the office and personnel sections, above, composed of aluminum, clear glass, frosted glass, and black glass; and by the delicate crystalline pavilion, far right, which serves as entrance to the store from the Lijnbaan mall. The catenary roof of the pavilion hangs from two reinforced concrete cantilevered beams which are supported on four central concrete columns.

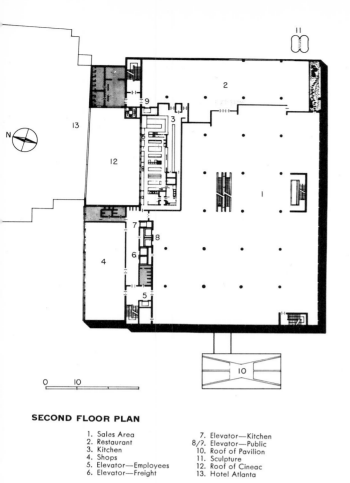

SECOND FLOOR PLAN

1. Sales Area
2. Restaurant
3. Kitchen
4. Shops
5. Elevator—Employees
6. Elevator—Freight
7. Elevator—Kitchen
8/9. Elevator—Public
10. Roof of Pavilion
11. Sculpture
12. Roof of Cineac
13. Hotel Atlanta

The striations in the travertine, left center, vary in direction to furnish texture and self-weathering; are calculated to let the stonework age gracefully.

From the second floor restaurant one looks out over the Henry Moore figure, at bottom, towards the 1930 store, designed by Willem Dudok.

Photo credits—Top: Spies, two at center: Robert Doisneau, Bottom: Frits Monshouwer

Above, one sees a main stairway, finished in travertine and with teak handrail. Typical interiors throughout are a well mannered combination of natural teak, travertine, light and dark gray, and cobalt blue — enlivened at each level by small areas or accents of orange-red.

For the sales areas, right, typical ceilings are composed of a suspended rectilinear pattern of wood members — teak for the ground floor and white painted wood above — which house fluorescent lighting panels and open to, yet conceal, the ducts and pipes (painted charcoal gray) above.

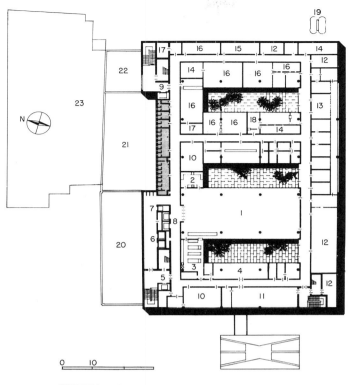

FOURTH FLOOR PLAN

1. Employees Dining	10. Instruction	18. Mail Room
2. Dishwashing	11. Workshop	19. Sculpture
3. Kitchen	12. Storage	20. Roof of Mechanical
4. Kitchen Storage	13. Conference Room	Section
5. Elevator—Employees	14. Records	21. Roof of Cinema
6. Elevator—Freight	15. Linen Room	22. Roof of Cinema Lobby
7. Elevator—Kitchen	16. Bookkeeping	23. Hotel Atlanta
8/9. Elevator—Public	17. Vault	

The employees' cafeteria and executive offices, at roof level, face out to garden-courts, one of which is shown directly below.

Point-of-sale fixtures, designed by architect Schwartzman, are shown in the three interior photos below. Left, china and glass department; right, cutlery department and wine shop.

The photograph on the page following is a view along the executive floor corridor.

Photos on pages 56, 58 and top of 57 by Spies; bottom of page 57 by Frits Monshouwer

TOWN HOUSE REMODELED INTO ATTRACTIVE GIFT SHOP

The 20th Century Shop, New Orleans, La. Burk, Le Breton and Lamantia, Architects; Barley, Inc., Civil Engineers and General Contractors.

This distinguished remodeling—winner of a first honor award at the Eighth Annual Conference of the Gulf States Region, A.I.A., succeeds in creating within the shell of an old town house a gift shop with an appealing character both contemporary and nostalgic.

In describing the process and result, architect James Lamantia says, "The problem was the complete transformation of an 1885 double town house into a shop for small gifts of high quality. The proximity of this house to its neighbors dictated the conditions that a similar scale should be preserved and that materials should be harmonious.

"The basic dimensions were therefore held intact—even to the alternate rhythm of vertical openings and blank wall area in the façade—although the building was virtually rebuilt, to the extent that even the outer skin was replaced.

"A second-level balcony was removed, along with most interior bearing walls, to be replaced by steel beams and split 'cradling' columns. A two-story well of space was created by cutting back the second floor to give the effect of a mezzanine as one enters.

"The old masonry of the side chimneys was exposed to accent further the verticality of the space, and to serve also as a reminder of the original structure."

All photos by Frank Lotz Miller

The 20th Century Shop

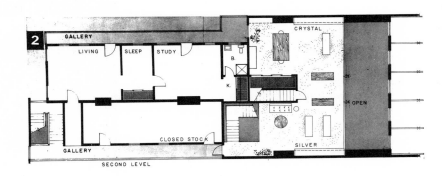

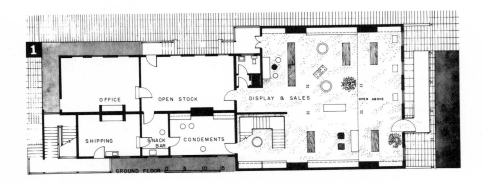

The difference in level between floor and sidewalk was turned from a liability into a capital gain by the attractive open ramp, which makes a strong point of interest in the façade. The projecting louver is porcelain-enameled steel in alternate beige and bone-white colors; stucco side panels act as baffles at either side of the front; painted diagonal cypress boarding sheathes the wall areas between openings; the sash is of natural aluminum.

The floors are finished with rubber or asphalt tile; the walls are variously plaster, walnut panels, or the old brick; acoustic tile is used on the ceilings

JAPANESE RETAILERS INVADE FIFTH AVENUE

All photos: Louis Reens, courtesy Owens-Corning Fiberglas Corp.

Takashimaya, Inc., New York. Steinhardt & Thompson, Architects; Junzo Yoshimura, Associated Architect; Robert P. Perillo, Mechanical Engineer; Lewin & Shapiro, Structural Engineers; Thomas Killian, Lighting Consultant; Charles Herman Co., General Contractors. Imported fixtures (1st and 2nd floors) by Shigeru Kawakami for Takashimaya Koshakusho, installed by Display Builders, Inc.

This effective remodeling—the first American branch of a Japanese department store chain—is notable for making its entire corner a two-story display; for successfully flouting a Fifth Avenue merchandising habit; but most importantly for creating in its three-story sales space an atmosphere peculiarly appropriate to store character and to the handsome, beautifully crafted (and expensive) Japanese merchandise. Inside, the total impression is of luxury and serenity—achieved physically by the quiet elegance of both goods and setting. The lighting is even; the walls are neutral or white; the carpeting is gray or tan; either light (hinoki) or dark (keyaki) natural wood makes a soft accent everywhere.

Placing the stair at the entrance—rather than further back in the store, only to be reached after passing tempting displays of impulse goods—is contrary to usual merchandising technique; but making a visual focus of the cherrywood and steel stair construction has created such an eye-catcher that visitors have far outnumbered expectations, and selling is brisk.

A garden under the stairway—arranged by David Engel—greets the visitor upon entering. The ground floor is then devoted to gifts, books, fabrics, etc.; the second floor to larger and more expensive items of metal, pottery, wood, and glass; the basement area features furniture, displayed under lighting of a domestic character.

The bottom right photo on the opposite page shows the garden under the stair; the other two picture the basement furniture sales area.

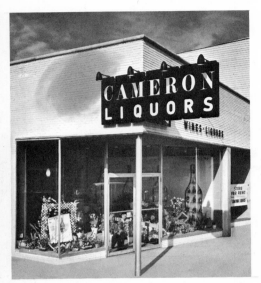

Cameron Liquor Store, Tarrytown, New York. Arthur Malsin and Don Reiman, Architects; Edward Schildback, Associate.

Joseph W. Molitor

ATMOSPHERE PLUS MAXIMUM DISPLAY OF GOODS

The image liquor stores try to present is of maximum stock, so the customer can purchase any familiar brand and also see others of which he has never heard. Prices are usually prominent in the display in order to make comparison shopping easy.

But a more subtle and important quality is atmosphere. Each of the shops shown here successfully creates its own air, yet one has a completely different feeling than the other. Both are attractive and successful.

The Cameron store (above) was an interior job within an existing shell and front. It has a closed-in, or inside, or wine-cellar look; furthered by the smart, curved ceiling of natural cypress. High-level lighting plus special shelving and cases with maple butcher-block tops and white uprights add to the general effect, which is inviting.

The Bottle Shop (right), on the other hand, opens up to the outside in California fashion to make the entire store a display. A gravel and planted strip next to the glass contributes to this effect. The lighting here is of a generally low level, with spots emphasizing the merchandise on display.

Morley Baer

The Bottle Shop, Inc., Sausalito, Cal. John G. Kelley, Architect; Dorothy Alexander, Project Manager.

Joseph W. Molitor

MERCHANDISING BY ARCHITECTURE AND GRAPHICS

Joseph W. Molitor

Carr's Department Store, West Orange, N. J. Katz Waisman Blumenkranz Stein Weber, Architects Associated; Constantino Nivola, Sculpture; Ladislav Sutnar, Graphics; Alfred Engel, Lighting Consultant.

Architect Richard G. Stein says, "This Carr's represents the trial run of a concept. We originally prepared a merchandising study for a self-service department store, combining our efforts with those of sculptor Nivola and graphics designer Sutnar. (see model photos below—Ed.). When plans were complete, lease negotiations fell through. In order to set up a prototype without delay, space was rented in the Essex Green Center, under construction.

"The job then was to apply the principles of the previous study to an existing space. Nivola designed sculpture (left) which was executed in porcelain enamel; Sutnar developed a new system of graphics.

"Since space is intensively used for merchandising, and department sizes must shift with the seasons, the flexibility of the fixtures has worked out well."

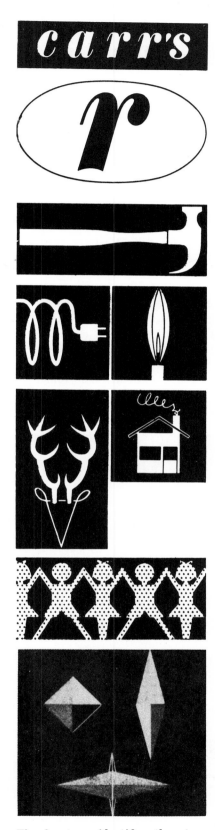

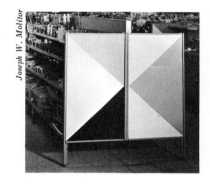

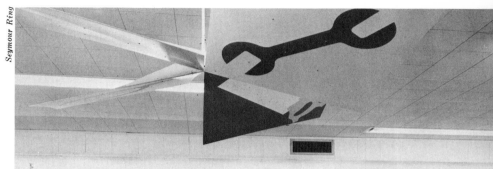

Seymour Ring

Joseph W. Molitor

Joseph W. Molitor

The logotype identifies the store from near and far; by day and by night. The symbols are used to identify merchandising departments, and combine with a color system (for counter ends and signs) to that end. Graphic design was carried through to include shopping bags, stationery, etc.

SWEDISH STORE WITH NOTABLE INTERIORS

Nordiska Kompaniet Store
Farsta Center, Stockholm, Sweden

ARCHITECTS: *Backstrom & Reinius*

INTERIOR ARCHITECT: *Hans Harald Molander*

CONSULTING ARCHITECTS: *Ketchum & Sharp*

All photos by Alexandre Georges

This air-conditioned department store—which serves a market of 235,000 in suburban Stockholm—was designed by a team of Swedish and American architects working in close collaboration. The result is that American store planning methods and merchandising concepts have shaped the building and determined its interiors, while Swedish design has given the whole its visual character. Unlike most Swedish stores, which combine natural and artificial light, Nordiska Companiet has blank upper walls and artificial light only, in accordance with American practice. Interiors are typically Swedish in character, with color sparingly used, and with white and natural wood serving as predominant tones.

At left, the façade on the center's main pedestrian mall. The upper walls and pierced balustrade are of textured gray Swedish granite; the store front glazing members are bronze; the exposed columns at ground level are clad in polished gray granite.

Ground floor sales area. White marble floor; natural walnut and white plastic sales fixtures

China and glassware department

China department

Lamp department

Women's sportswear section

Women's shoe department

Tearoom on the upper floor

TWO-LEVEL STORE: TWO-LEVEL PARKING

The Hecht Company
Marlow Heights, Maryland

ARCHITECTS & ENGINEERS:
Abbott, Merkt & Co.

ASSOCIATE ARCHITECT:
Daniel Schwartzman

GENERAL CONTRACTOR:
Prescott Construction Co.

Regarding the design of this visually exciting branch department store in suburban Washington, architect Daniel Schwartzman says, "The lower level has direct access to the shopping center mall on one side; while the upper level has access to a secondary mall to be built later. This split level arrangement provides direct access to parking on both levels. One of the design problems was to solve, as gracefully as possible, the relationship between the two entrances at different levels. Our solution was an open reinforced concrete stairway with a curved canopy, connecting the two arched canopies which shelter, respectively, the lower walkway and the upper entrance.

"The structure is of reinforced concrete, and where it remained exposed it was given a liquid tile finish in off-white. Major exterior walls were faced with split-face, exposed quartz aggregate concrete brick, also off-white. Large panels of precast, exposed quartz aggregate concrete in sculptured form—large in scale—were used for the panels over the entrances (shown in the photograph below). The simple and rather elegant quality achieved by the single color of the building, together with its arched and sculptured forms, gives it a distinctive character expression of the merchandising philosophy of the store."

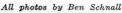
All photos by Ben Schnall

The Hecht Company

View at lower level corner, showing arcaded display windows and open stairs to upper level

China and glassware department has interesting see-through character, due to coordination of fixtures and building

Exterior view of the china and glassware department, located at the lower level corner shown at left

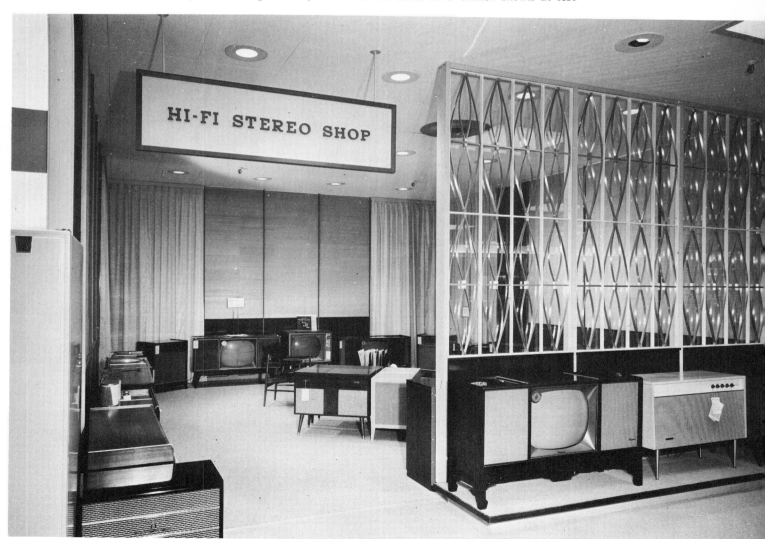

A decorative metal grill separates and defines the Hi-Fi and television department as a small shop

ON UPPER FIFTH AVENUE: WALLACHS' LARGEST

All photos © Ezra Stoller

ARCHITECTS: *Ketchum, Giná & Sharp*

ENGINEERS: *Syska & Hennessy*

CONTRACTORS: *Hinzmann & Waldmann*

Fᴏʀ ᴛʜɪs — the largest and most elegant of Wallachs eleven men's stores — several ideas guided the design. Their soundness has been demonstrated by large sales volume.

THE FRONT was made open by floor-to-ceiling glass and free-standing displays. After tramping over most of mid-town Manhattan to observe men's shops, Architect Frank Giná decided such a scheme (more common to women's stores) would be good business for Wallachs. The 125 ft spread — longest of any 5th Avenue men's store — creates an impressive effect, both by day and night.

COLOR is the big news in men's clothing; so why not make the merchandise the center of attraction, the store itself a neutral foil? This was done by using gray terrazzo, off-white painted plaster, and natural woods for floor, ceiling, walls, fixtures. The only color plane at street level lies behind the cashier's desk (bottom) where there is no merchandise display.

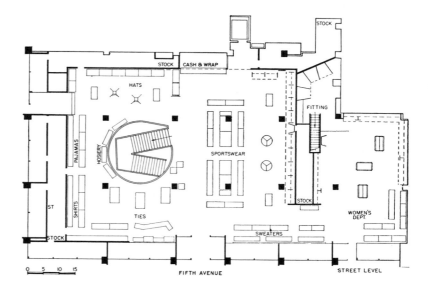

THE WAY SPACE IS HANDLED unites ground floor and lower level, thus removing from the latter the old-fashioned "basement" implication and making it first rate sales area. The interesting central stair, architectural feature, is designed to that end; the tying-together effect is furthered by the flat-domed lighting recess above.

Visual unity stems also from the free arrangement of the low fixtures, which do not create directional aisles and which nowhere rise above eye level to block one's view of the entire area.

FIXTURES were designed to bring merchandise into the open, free for customer inspection — calculated to spark impulse sales. They are typically of plastic, glass, or natural wood, supported by slender metal frames. Similar frames, wall hung, decoratively serve as stock shelves in the lower level shoe department (bottom photo).

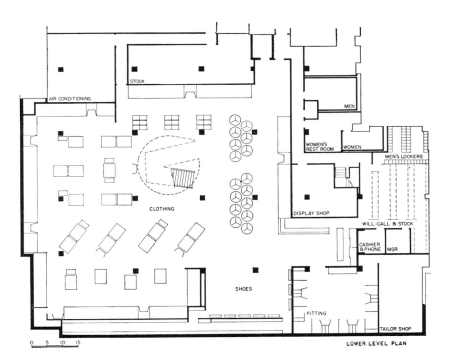

LOWER LEVEL PLAN

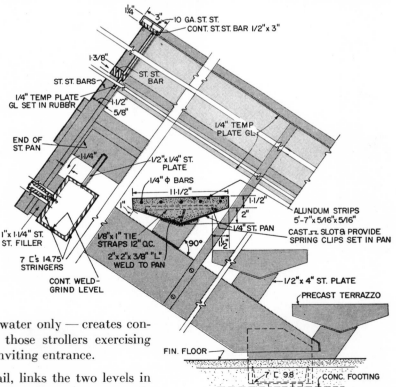

THE DOG BAR— for city water only — creates conversation; practically forces those strollers exercising canines to pause beside the inviting entrance.

THE STAIR, shown in detail, links the two levels in sprightly fashion. The light gray precast terrazzo treads (with non-slip inserts) are supported by lemon yellow painted steel runners. The ¼ in. tempered glass balustrade is topped by a stainless steel handrail. At lower level the flight lands on a square of vinyl tile, the remainder of this area being carpeted.

BOLD GEOMETRY AND GLASS FOR AUTO SALES

Thomson Brothers Cadillac Agency, Cincinnati, Ohio

Architects & Engineers: A. M. Kinney Associates
John R. Morris, Project Manager
Charles Burchard, Director of
Architecture

Landscape Architect: Eleanor A. Christie
Interior Designer: Harbine Chatfield
Contractor: Charles V. Maescher & Co.

THERE IS cliché danger in the ill-considered use of the glass box. There is also — in the right situation — the opportunity to make of it a glowing, crystal showplace for business that evokes comment; ups sales. Here, at night, against the small, broken-up patches of light characteristic of Cincinnati's environment, the bold geometry of this stainless steel cage and its strip lighting come alive to make a striking display visible for some distance along Gilbert Avenue. For daytime effect, the glass cube, topped by light blue porcelain panels, is played interestingly against long horizontal ribbons of sand colored brick and corrugated aluminum enclosing service and used car areas to the rear. Planted courts placed at "hinge points" in the plan contrast nicely to the severity of the building; enable one to view the cars on display against a natural background.

Three main elements comprise the plan: the showroom, sales and office group fronting on the principal

Bill Engdahl, Hedrich-Blessing

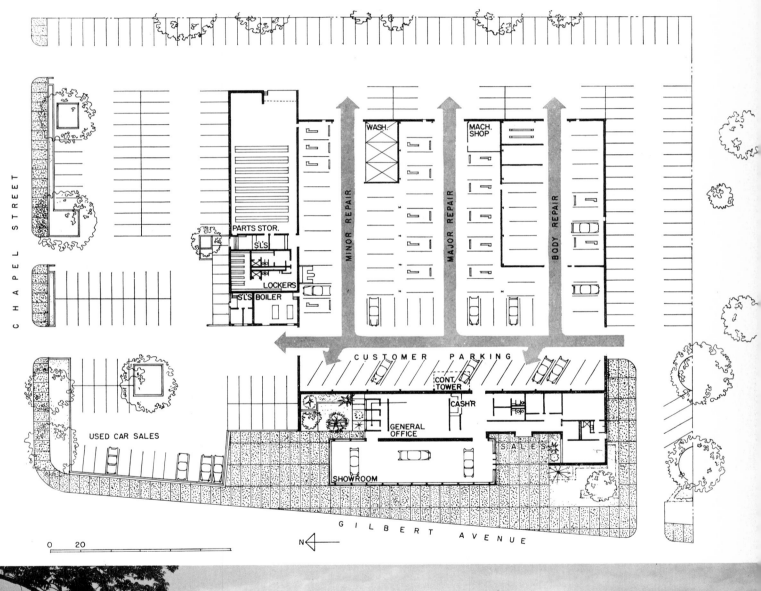

CHAPEL STREET

PARTS STOR.

SL'S

LOCKERS

SL'S BOILER

MINOR REPAIR

WASH.

MAJOR REPAIR

MACH. SHOP

BODY REPAIR

CUSTOMER PARKING

CONT. TOWER

CASH'R

GENERAL OFFICE

SALES

USED CAR SALES

SHOWROOM

0   20

N

GILBERT AVENUE

President's office

Office reception area

Bill Engdahl, Hedrich-Blessing

Sales conference room

Offices for closing sales

street; the service area immediately behind, reached by a private driveway; and the used car and parts department, approached from a minor street through a parking area. This area embraces an outside display space for used cars which faces on the principal street.

The service area is framed within 20 by 70 ft bays, providing a clear space with but two rows of columns. The latter define the three-way function of the department and help channel its traffic — controlled by a tower in much the same fashion as airport traffic. This area is designed for possible future expansion eastward, as is the flanking parts department which serves it.

Office and sales area interiors were the subject of a great deal of study, as the photographs above indicate. The results are especially noteworthy for a building devoted to automobile sales and service.

The basic structure is a steel skeleton with metal roof deck. The exterior is faced with brick, corrugated aluminum or porcelain enamel panels over concrete block; service area sash are steel, industrial type; the overhead garage doors are motor controlled. The service area is finished in glazed structural tile; the office area wall finishes are generally painted plaster or face brick, with portions wood panelled. Floors in the front portion are ceramic tile, quarry tile or asphalt tile; ceilings are acoustic tile or painted plaster.

TWO SEARS STORES IN THE SOUTHEAST

1. Sears Roebuck & Company, Memphis, Tennessee

A. L. Aydelott & Associates
Architects

These two stores—while different in size and situation—none the less have in common the architectural problem of organizing, articulating, and enclosing a series of given sales spaces upon a given portion of the plot, with a set relationship between departments and a designated flow pattern between entrances and vertical circulation; all in general accordance with a set of schematics prepared by the owner's planning department. The Memphis store is one of two in suburban locations that serve that city; the Pine Bluff unit caters to an entire community of 40,000.

The exteriors—important in attracting the suburban motorist or pedestrian—have been handled with a degree of style and imagination. In both cases the regularity of the exposed, painted steel frame sets up a basic rectilinear pattern against which the surfaces, texture, and color of the panel infilling treatment offer an interesting counterplay.

For the garden and farm sales area, textured pierced brick and gates
of wrought iron lend a felicitous scale and character not common to a
store containing 16,000 sq. ft

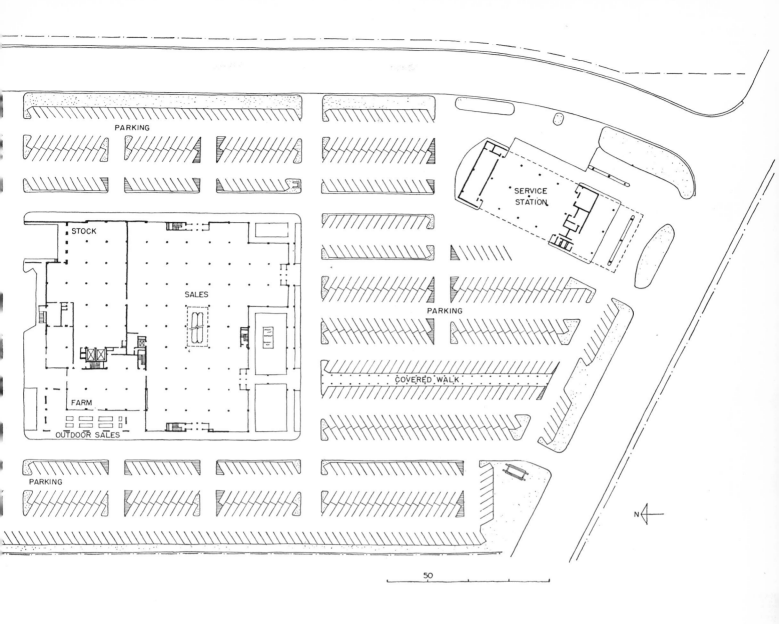

PARKING

STOCK

SALES

FARM

OUTDOOR SALES

PARKING

SERVICE STATION

PARKING

COVERED WALK

N

50

The infilling—consisting of 9 by 20 ft precast panels—builds up an effective in-and-out texture of patterned rectangles. Blue gray terra-cotta bands at top and bottom tie together the various high and low elements of the scheme in neat fashion.

The third floor penthouse, devoted to offices and services, is enclosed by five barrel vaults that provide a gracefully undulating contrast to the rectilinearity of the main mass. The motif is repeated in the service station unit.

2. Sears Roebuck & Company, Pine Bluff, Arkansas

The infilling panels for the Pine Bluff store are of ceramic mosaic tile arranged in a concave trapezoidal pattern. The tile setting bed is supported on metal lath within steel frames, which are left exposed and painted to become part of the exterior design. The combination of panels, matte black structural steel members, carefully placed lettering, and the local yellow-flecked red brick creates a striking effect that is popular with both town folk and store personnel. The owners say "the store is doing well."

A. L. Aydelott & Associates Architects

Presented with the problem of combining a two-story office and service element running the length of the building with an adjoining one-story sales space, the architect raised the ceiling of the sales area, used the 7-ft truss space for ducts, electrical and mechanical facilities, and came up with a clean, well organized parallelepiped as the enclosing form for the entire store and its services.

With the exception of the exterior finishes, the construction and materials for the two stores are similar. Both are steel framed with roof slabs of lightweight insulating concrete; interior walls are painted plaster; floors are terrazzo; ceilings are finished with acoustic tile. Both stores are completely air-conditioned, and lighted by a combination of incandescent and fluorescent fixtures

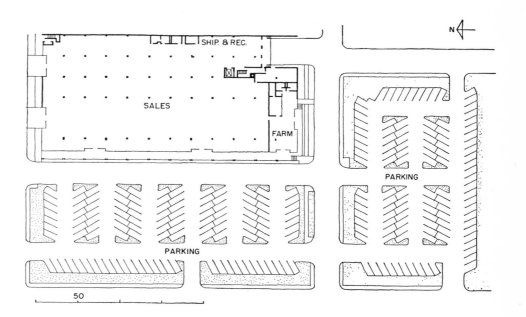

N

SHIP. & REC.

SALES

FARM

PARKING

PARKING

50

The service station, an important element in every Sears retail store, had to be located in this case across the street. However, the essential character of the larger store was carefully maintained in the design of the smaller unit

A view of the principle facade as seen in sharp perspective below, emphasizes the three dimensional aspect of the trapezoidal patterns in the exterior panels, which are 20 by 25 ft, with a maximum concavity of 2 ft

SHOPPING CENTERS

© *Ezra Stoller*

Suburban Shopping Can Be a Pleasure

Suburban shopping *can be* a pleasant experience, but seldom is. Great numbers of shopping centers are being built across the country, but the unhappy truth is that the overwhelming majority of them are neither good to look at nor a real pleasure to use. The American genius for turning a profit seems, in suburbia, to be wedded to a distressing penchant for bringing merchandising blight to the land as part of the process. In terms of logic, convenience, or visual delight, the typical shopping center offers little. Occasional exceptions, such as the centers presented in this section, demonstrate by contrast the validity of this judgment. Shopping *can be* a pleasure!

There have been good results from the large amount of study devoted to the location, planning, and servicing of retail stores; and their grouping into a smoothly functioning center that performs as a profitable mechanism for sales. But there has been far less accomplishment in the design of the spaces between and around these stores; their parking areas; the relationship of such centers to the highway and the community; in brief—the *shopping environment*. This is the aspect of shopping center design that can make the difference. Only when more owners appreciate the importance of such an environment and the unique role of the architect in achieving it can large numbers of shopping areas benefit in both financial and human terms. Each of the twelve shopping centers we present in this section makes a significant contribution in the direction of a delightful climate for shopping.

– J.S.H.

CONTROL OF GRAPHICS ESSENTIAL TO GOOD SHOPPING CENTER DESIGN

Architect Edward Larrabee Barnes explains
how his concept for the new Neiman Marcus Center
will insure a unified architecture for shopping

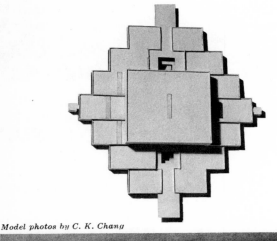

Model photos by C. K. Chang

Plan and perspective views of a model to study the massing of the Neiman Marcus Center, Fort Worth, Texas (see text)

The major obstacle to good architecture in shopping centers is the sign. One cannot plan for chaos, yet that is what the shopping center architect is asked to do—produce a unified design while the landlord capitulates to tenant sign demands. The pattern is typical across the country. There are many examples of attractive courtyards, Miesian details, and canopies over which a good architect has sweated to no avail; for in the end all one really sees is the clash of conflicting advertising, with each tenant trying to shout louder than the next.

A good shopping center is impossible without an enlightened, understanding developer; one who wants unified architecture. The budget for site and buildings must be economically sound, for even the most understanding developer will capitulate to tenant demands if rentals are slow. There must be agreement by all involved that the identity of this market place is more important than the identity of the various individual tenants.

We are fortunate enough to be working on such a job. The enlightened, understanding developer is

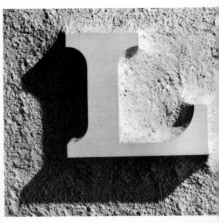

Cherry Hill

Left to right: graphic devices for several of the centers covered in this section: Cherry Hill, page 164; New England, page 170; The Mall at Short Hills, page 160

Neiman Marcus; the site is in Fort Worth, between two growing shopping boulevards. And there is an agreement that the shopping complex shall make a single, strong architectural statement.

The unity of the Neiman Marcus center can be seen in the plan and perspective at left. The department store—the drawing card—is surrounded by smaller stores. There are open courtyard entrances from the main streets and side entrances from the flanking parking lots. Basically, the parent store has willingly permitted itself to be surrounded by a cluster of shops. Since the site slopes, the complex will appear almost as a village, with individual shops at different levels and the Neiman Marcus two-story block rising in the center.

Such an integrated design obviously requires great discipline in the use of materials and signs. The total impact must count, and not become lost in a fringe of fratricidal competition. The solution is simple: all walls of rough white stucco, all signs of raised white letters. The tenant logotype is of deep ribbon Venus letters in white porcelain enamel; the department store lettering grows from the walls, the stucco curving out boldly to flat, smooth faces. Everything is white on white. At night, lights will throw the sculptured surfaces into bold relief; during the day the Texas sun will create a continuously changing play of light and shadow.

Where does this treatment throw the emphasis? From the nearby highways the total architecture counts, making a massive statement that can withstand the competition of gas stations, motels, etc. As one walks about the building or through the courts, the merchandise and planting will count. The continuous white stucco surfaces will set off the contents of the shopping center as the white background sets off the advertising photographer's model. On the Greek island of Mykonos the continuous white walls and roofs and pavements of the village dramatize the ikon in the church or a geranium in a window. Here—on a commercial level—the same principle of continuity will apply. The architecture will become a background for activity.

—EDWARD LARRABEE BARNES

All photos by Joseph W. Molitor except where otherwise noted

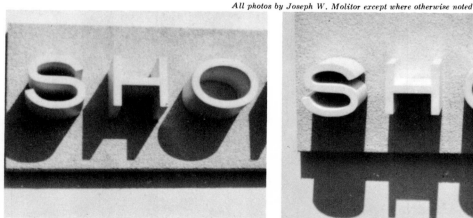

PLANNING SHOPPING CENTERS FOR PEDESTRIANS

*by Richard M. Bennett**

SHOPPING IS DEFINED as "looking at, pricing, or buying merchandise displayed for sale."

While the success of a shopping center is measured by the magnitude of the buying therein, one must not forget that — varying with the type of merchandise — the *looking at* and the *pricing* are the foundation of the *buying* act.

Foodstuffs, laundry items and other standard things used every day — widely advertised and with narrow price variations — can be sold in a Buying Center. Here, the main design problem is easy and convenient access to demand merchandise — essential items which *must* be bought periodically. Once attracted, the captive buyer can then be exposed to impulse items which, when *looked at,* are often purchased, if the *pricing* is attractive.

On the other hand "Big Ticket" merchandise (more expensive and important) demands different handling, and here is the real difference between a Shopping Center and a Buying Center; for being bigger is only one factor. A Shopping Center is a place where one goes to seek, to look at, to find, compare, price and buy, and the implication of the adventure of finding is an important ingredient.

On Shopping Itself

Looked at in broader terms, Shopping is a Social Ritual. The wife and homemaker charged with the wise spending of the family income must be given the sense that she has *worked* at seeking out and discovering a uniquely right article at a justifiable price.

It is not enough to have important purchases merely available. They must be as available as possible but in an atmosphere that suggests the culmination of a quest.

A Shopping Center can, and should have a number of terminal atmospheres. For example, one appliance selling area could be bright, overwhelming in range of stock and suggesting that things must be cheap because there are so many of them. Another location could display the same products with different lighting and greater spacing so that quality is stressed and the uniquenesses and features of products emphasized.

Above all, the opportunity must be given to *compare.* What can one get for a little more — or a little less money? Does one want the red one — or should one take the sensible black one? What does the other store have — how does it differ?

The larger shopping center is relatively more successful today because it can offer a deeper selection of merchandise at a wider range of prices than is possible in a smaller center.

Actually, shopping centers are not an entirely new phenomenon. A glance backward in history and some off-beat observations at other less recognized

* Who also made these delightfully spontaneous sketches in the margins of a rough draft, with no idea they would be published. (Ed.)

merchandising arrangements might be stimulating in evaluating the present — and in looking ahead.

Village Plans

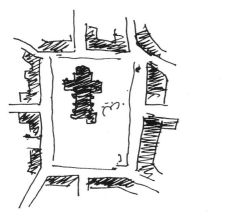

Thomas Sharp, the English Town Planner, tracing the development of the English Village through obvious crossroad, ferry and Roman legionary camp origins, failed to discover a village along a simple, straight road. Surprisingly, though, there *are* villages established along curved roads when the curvature is such that one cannot look *through* the settlement.

Towns built around open squares, often stemming from the Roman occupation, are interesting in that very often the advent of Christianity found the church built in a corner or end of the open space so that it terminated the principal streets leading to the square. Perhaps more importantly the church or cathedral site prevented views *out* of the square. There is evidence, too, that other streets leading outward were allowed to bend and curve so as not to invite one to leave the center. For the merchants with shops ringing the square, the church obviously blocks a number of views towards their individual establishments, but this is more than offset by the fact that when one is near their shops there is less distraction from other stores. The attention of potential customers tends to be concentrated upon the nearest shops.

Amusement Parks

Though a neglected chapter in architectural history, amusement parks are excellent merchandising complexes because most people spend more than they intend in these ingenious layouts. The typical arrangement seems to be a meandering closed ring which returns on itself so that one starts a second circuit before one realizes it. While at first glance the informal layout may appear "Parklike" in character, the looking-around-a-corner process lures one forward and — at the same time — by shortening and limiting the view, as in many villages, concentrates one's attention upon the attractions most nearly at hand.

In pondering about the principles behind such plans, Coney Island, remembered as stretching straight along a beach, seemed to be a disconcerting exception. It is, of course, one of the most famous and successful of all amusement centers.

A trip there to check shows that it is not in reality built along a straight line, but is a great curved walk skirting a bay. As one promenades, the vista directly ahead is always dominated by shops and views into attractions.

One cannot help wonder what would have happened if the beach had been built on an outside curve around a headland instead of along a bay.

The famous Atlantic City boardwalk follows the same merchandising principles as Coney Island.

Carnivals

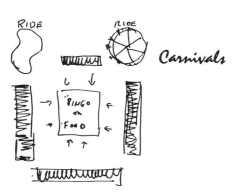

Much as amusement parks, carnivals are high-powered merchandising endeavors. Since they are assembled every week or so at different locations with changing components, they have a flexibility of arrangement that is responsive to practical experience. Conversations with carnival operators indicate that they are usually set up following the same principles as amusement parks, with a central attraction ringed by booths and secondary attractions including the "rides" in the corners. The central feature is such that it can be approached from all sides, and varies from a Bingo Tent to some sort of food concession.

Department Stores

The highly developed interior planning of department stores may seem haphazard at first glance but the change of pace, space and direction — the informal arrangement — represents hard-headed thinking and experience. If certain principles work within the store, then they must have application to the spaces *between* buildings if the shopping adventure is to be a unified, total experience.

Streets—The Limited View

Could it be that most great shopping streets curve, bend, are short, or somehow establish limited views? For example, the Rue de Rivoli is straight but the massive piers of the enclosing arcade minimize the distraction of street traffic and the neighboring park.

One of the most entrancing and pleasant of shopping streets is Copenhagen's Stroget. Narrow and charming, it changes its name as it bends; opens occasionally into a square; presents a succession of visual changes. As one succumbs to the adventure, there is never a vista too far for understanding, and one finds himself hoping the street will never end.

Fifth Avenue in New York is a most famous shopping street — yet it is straight and it is successful — but is it? Actually, it has hardly settled down and has been travelling uptown these many years seeking a fixed point; some stabilizing element. Maybe the cross-axis at Radio City and the end-of-the-line at Central Park will stop its travel. We should realize that its success as a shopping area is probably based on the presence of many people who are there for a purpose other than shopping — such as business or sight-seeing. Our new regional shopping centers must, by the nature of their situation, create their own attraction.

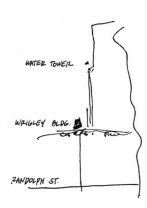

Then there are streets with limited views and the smell of adventure which are not great successes as shopping streets — as yet. For example, Chicago's North Michigan Avenue is an attractive thoroughfare, especially when contrasted to its southern extension. Looking north from Randolph Street one's view is blocked by the Wrigley Building. Arriving near it and the Chicago River one jogs a little east and again the view is blocked, this time by the Old Water Tower. Again, jogging past that, the street stretches on until it opens into the lakefront. Its fascination is such that a walk along it is never tiring and one is apt to follow it further than he intended. Its potential as a shopping street is unrealized because of unused sites and lack of concentration.

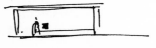

Scale

Architectural scale plays a most important part in relating customer and merchandise. It is sometimes difficult for architects to remember that a piece of architecture — the building — should be considered as a frame for the picture of the love affair between a customer and a piece of merchandise. When the frame is too big, the customer is apt to feel that both she and the merchandise are inadequate — too small — to consummate the attachment.

The Future

As more large Shopping Centers are constructed and they begin to compete, which will be successful? Price competition, quality of merchandise competition, operational economies, and so on are important factors. But for the designer, all other things being equal, might it not be true that the architectural solution most sensitive to the psychological and social needs of the customers will have a final edge? Is this a lesson from the past and other contemporary merchandising plans?

The present day sees one disciplined straight-line mall or open strip development after another, most of them fairly successful. They tell all about themselves as soon as possible, and all the merchants are given an even break. Such schemes are rational, successful, convenient, efficient, smart, fashionable — but how many show human understanding and a love of adventure?

It remains to be seen whether or not the limited view, more attention to human scale, the lure of around-the-corner, the conscious creation of a sense of adventure will contribute to — or even be necessary for — the success of the evolving American Shopping Center. I think they will.

Drawing by Richard Jennings

RETAILING AND THE AUTOMOBILE

Editor's Introduction

Trapped in a slow-moving, vehicular highway chain, or sitting bumper-to-bumper in the choking, angry snarl of Anycity traffic, we sometimes wish all those cars and trucks and busses would just go away. But, unlike the amiable snowman—who must one day melt away to nothing—the motor vehicle is here to stay. And if both business and pleasure are to benefit from it, the only course is to design (or redesign) *both* buildings and their settings—the city, the suburb, the countryside—so that pedestrians, vehicles, and public transport can each move freely and expeditiously without becoming entangled or spoiling the looks and pleasantness of things, or without disrupting the processes of government and business and living.

In the following article we consider design for retailing; but especially in the light of its relationship to the automobile, the person on foot, and the environment in which it occurs. For retailing is no longer confined to the city or town market place as it used to be; thanks to the automobile, it takes place everywhere—in the city, in the suburbs, on the open highway.

Architectural design for retailing must therefore revolve about the situation of the building or buildings, and a studied examination and plan for the movement and accommodation of all kinds of traffic inside, outside, and around the building; and also in the neighborhood and community involved. A more general concern for the retailing environment can lead to—and in many cases has—a broadening of the architect's influence into such activities as urban redevelopment, neighborhood planning, regional planning, and so on.

With cities beginning to fight back in an effort to recapture some of the business lost to suburbia and regain their place as retailing centers, the downtown shopping center—a new building type—looms large as one to watch, and appears to offer all sorts of opportunities for architects and engineers. This is not to discount the suburban center, which will continue to have a rightful place in retailing's future and offer opportunities also; the point is that good design for each kind of retailing will create the special parti most appropriate for its particular situation.

—J.S.H.

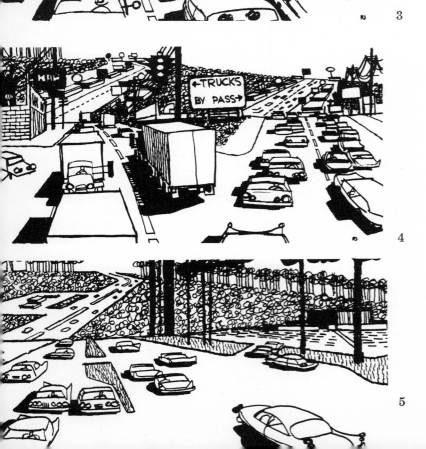

The desecration of the countryside,
and a possible way of redemption;
a series by Richard Jennings:
1—The Forest Primeval
2—The First Highway
3—Plus Highway Merchandising
4—Plus More Traffic; Today
5—A Way Out—Planned Retailing; 19—?

RETAILING AND

A ROMANCE BASED UPON

by Victor Gruen

In the past thirty years, retailing has
been strongly influenced by the automobile; and as we find so often in history, romance played a part in the story.
A love affair developed between the retailer and the automobile, creating a
desire in the retailer to be as close as possible to the object of his affection. Although the first bloom of this romance
has now faded, many retailers still have
a lingering feeling that they would like
to be close to the automobile. Let us
briefly review the development of retailing and see how this affair began.

Richard Jennings

THE AUTOMOBILE

A CASE OF MISTAKEN IDENTITY

Prologue*

Buying and selling is as old as mankind. Prehistoric man exchanged the deer he had slain for a necklace of shells; the modern housewife acquires a package of frozen food in exchange for money—the gratification of needs or desires motivated each transaction. Only the conditions under which each transpired have changed. A condition of great importance was the appearance of the middleman—the merchant—who turned this gratification into commerce. He carried the work produced by others from place to place; he established trade routes and trading posts; he started country stores and merchant states. Wherever he settled he became an integral, invigorating part of the life around him.

In ancient Greece, the merchant spread his wares beneath the colonnades of a building especially designated for his activity, the *Stoa*. The *Stoa* was no less important in the *Agora* (or city square) than the *Bouleuterion*, where politicians met, or the *Ecclesiasterion*, designed for public meetings. The temple was nearby, citizens in the square discussed topics of the day, transacted business, did their marketing. Buying and selling occurred where the philosophers, poets, and entertainers were arguing, reciting, performing their arts. Court trials were held here; banquets were spread. The *Agora* was the center of city life—and in this colorful, lively, dynamic environment commerce had its place. This integration of human activity was a universal pattern. Its existence was later guaranteed in ancient Rome, where wheeled traffic was banned from the city's forum when the vehicles threatened to crowd out humans.

---

*Although the main body of this article was written by Mr. Gruen especially for ARCHITECTURAL RECORD, the Prologue was condensed from a book by Victor Gruen and Larry Smith, SHOPPING TOWNS U.S.A., Reinhold Publishing Corp., 1960.

Top, the Stoa, *or open square, the Greek market place of classic times. Immediately above, a view of the market square in Leipzig, Germany, with vendors' stalls set up for business and with goods on display as in medieval times*

The problem of proper planning for pedestrian and automotive traffic; the confusion of a typical Main Street; the hazards—both by day and by night—of the shopping "strip," with cars parked, cars moving, cars trying to park; the displeasing impersonality of parking by the acre. These are the problems all too familiar to everyone everywhere; problems that cry out for a sensible and a pleasing solution

In the medieval city, the market square was the city's center, not only geographically, but socially, commercially, religiously, and culturally. The City Hall and Guild Hall were there, as was the cathedral, with merchants' and craftsmen's stalls about it. The open area in the center became, in turn, the market place, the fairground, and the entertainment center for the citizenry.

Our own New England villages centered on the village green—a concept our forefathers brought with them from Europe. Such greens—a pleasant focus for community life—persisted well into the 19th century.

The industrial revolution radically changed the organization and character of cities, where factories were built and men were sought to work in them. The machine proved to have an insatiable appetite for manpower, and the city grew into a crazy quilt of packed humanity. The industrial slum became a

new pattern in many cities. Life in such cities became almost intolerable, and those who could afford it led the march to the suburbs. The march increased its tempo with the advent of interurban, elevated, and subway trains—became a rout when the automobile appeared.

The automobile destroyed the last vestiges of community coherence. As long as tracks were the carriers of suburban dwellers, the new suburban communities had a central point—the railway station—to focus upon. As cities reached fingers out along the tentacles of railway lines, the shops, churches, and public buildings of the new towns sprang up about the station; and residential areas were controlled in their spread by walking distance. Such subcenters still exist in the Greater London Area.

When the automobile emerged as a means of private mass transportation, the final urban explosion took place. Automobiles provided complete freedom

Wide World Photos

of movement, and made the individual completely independent of public transportation.

To accommodate the flood of people seeking to escape from the city and find peace and beauty in the country, house builders tore up the ground, cut down the trees, and callously removed every vestige of what people were after. Modern suburbia was born; a *milieu* in which there were neither the values of a rural community nor those of a well planned urban environment. But people must live somewhere, and suburbia grew. According to the United States Census Bureau, suburbs grew 29 times as fast as central cities between 1950 and 1959. The rate of population increase in those years was 1.5 per cent in cities; 44 per cent in suburban areas. In 1957 New York City held a special census in an attempt to obtain additional state assistance by proving increased population. To the dismay of city officials, it was found that the population of the five boroughs

had *decreased* 1.2 per cent; and this at a time when the population of the surrounding Greater Metropolitan Area was dramatically increasing!

Distances between residential and downtown areas increased rapidly, yet public transportation faced the threat of annihilation. The inroads automobile travel has made on public transportation is indicated in a study made by the Westchester County Association, which shows that despite a population increase of 15.5 per cent from 1949 to 1954, the number of railroad commuters decreased during the same period by 16.3 per cent.

Throughout the United States, suburban growth was so rapid and frenzied that the construction of roads, highways, and lines for drainage, sewerage, power, and gas lagged years behind—while any serious attempt at good planning for schools, shopping facilities, community centers, and churches was virtually nonexistent. Row upon row of identical houses

Top, the octagonal Galleria of King Victor Emmanuel in Milan, Italy—an early and charming example of a covered mall for pedestrians. Immediately above, the old Cleveland Arcade, extending from Euclid to Superior Avenue, in Cleveland

R. Wenkam

set in an empty countryside proved to be less than the heaven their owners were seeking.

Since suburbia is having a marked effect upon our way of life, it is only natural that its influence should be felt in the marketing of goods. In the amorphous suburban environment, the merchant has had difficulty in finding a logical way to integrate his activities into the local scene. Stores were not provided with predetermined locations such as near the railway stations as in an earlier period—the customer no longer had a geographical focus; he and his car were everywhere. Under such conditions, the best retailing locations seemed centered on highways.

As an increasing number of highway stores appeared, more people parked along the curb and parking space became scarce. A new type of hitching post—the parking meter—made its appearance. But it cost money, and as the cost of curb parking tended to slow down sales, merchants responded and arranged for customer off-street parking; first in back of, and later in front of the stores.

Business grew, and so did traffic confusion. Highway congestion resulted—so serious in nature that motorists chose alternate, less crowded routes. When the alternate roads in turn attracted new stores and new congestion, superhighways were constructed to provide an unhindered traffic flow. Residential areas surrounding congested traffic arteries or situated near the stores or their services became undesirable; and the stores then found themselves in the center of a blighted residential section of reduced buying power. As customers were siphoned off from settled roads—partly by the appearance of blight and partly by the attraction of the freeways—a wild scramble for new locations started. Stores were built in freshly created suburban areas still further removed from downtown. Ironically enough, the merchants again encountered the same undesirable

Infinity, Inc.

Ewing Galloway

CONCERN FOR THE PEDESTRIAN

Above, the mall of the Cross County Shopping Center in Yonkers, N. Y., designed by architect Lathrop Douglass. Left, the mall of the Ala Moana Regional Shopping Center in Honolulu, Hawaii, designed by architects John Graham and Company.

Right, top, the access bridge serving the Gulfgate Shopping Center in Houston, Texas, designed by architects John Graham and Company. Immediately right, a bus stop and protected bus terminal and waiting room for the Southdale Shopping Center, Edina, Minnesota—near Minneapolis—designed by Victor Gruen Associates, architects. Both city and suburban busses serve the center

situation from which they were trying to escape. The need for farsighted, comprehensive planning became urgent and more widely understood at last.

When environmental planning is applied in designing new retailing facilities, the needs and desires of the shopper are involved. It is significant that the common name is *shopping center,* not *selling center.* This clearly indicates that the desires of the shopper take precedence over those of the retailer. An earlier term, *parking center,* failed to catch on.

Suburban shoppers require a convenient, amply stocked shopping area served by plentiful free parking. These are the purely practical needs about which the shopping center was first conceived. However, good planning will provide additional attractions by meeting other needs. By offering facilities for social life, recreation, civic and educational func-

tions within a protected pedestrian environment, shopping centers can fill an existing void. In the shopping centers that fulfill this need of suburbanites for the amenities, we find that pedestrian areas are busy not only during normal shopping hours, but that people promenade, windowshop, relax in the garden courts, view exhibits, and patronize the restaurants on Sundays and holidays. All age groups are considered; auditoriums are booked to capacity; meeting rooms are busy; dance and music schools and skating rinks attract teenagers. The amusement centers are popular with children.

Such a concept results in an upgrading of the surrounding residential area and raises property values. When the shopping center becomes indeed a place which provides physical living requirements for suburbia, and simultaneously fulfills civic, cultural, social, and recreational needs, it will make a significant contribution to better living.

Michael Honos

George E. Kawamoto

Gordon Sommers

CLUSTER-TYPE REGIONAL CENTERS

These three examples by Victor Gruen Associates illustrate the cluster-type regional shopping center, which has become—by now—a well established expression which has been built in various parts of the country by developers and their architects. Its typical features include an outer-ring road, ample parking, underground service, a department store or two as a "main draw," plus mall and plaza areas devoted strictly to pedestrians.

Top—Northland, near Detroit; Center—Eastland, near Detroit; Bottom—Valley Fair, San Jose, California

The main shopping mall, Wildwood Shopping Center, West Allis, Wisconsin—a two-story volume enclosed by precast concrete units, designed by Victor Gruen Associates, Architects

THE COVERED MALL

The Galleria of King Umberto I, in Naples, Italy—a prototype

The air conditioned garden court and some typical shops at Southdale Center, Minneapolis—designed by Victor Gruen Associates. In this controlled atmosphere, the conventional store "front" ceases to exist; and only a security barrier and some means of identification remain as required elements in the design

Disenchantment

As the retailer-automobile honeymoon comes to an end, the retailer slowly realizes that his love has been misdirected. His true love belonged not to the automobile, but to the female customer in it. No automobile—not even the most elegant Cadillac—ever bought a thing. As the retailer transferred his attachment from the car to the lady, he drew the logical conclusions which were then expressed by changes in store design and center planning.

Early automobile-conscious stores featured carriage trade entrances, but it was soon evident that the chauffeur-driven car was *passé* and that parking space had to be provided for the lady shopper. At first, stores were strung along the highway; the housewife drove from store to store, parking near front entrances and shopping as she went. When this became popular, parking space became scarce, and the highways became so congested that mobility for shopping—or for any other purpose—no longer existed.

Parking lots were next provided *behind* the stores. Shops and stores continued to present their "fronts" to the highway, but 90 per cent of their customers now came in by the back door—the same entrance through which garbage was removed and deliveries made.

The first planning step forward was taken when store buildings were moved back from the road and larger parking areas were provided in front. Now—for the first time—service facilities (at the back) and customer facilities (at the front) could be decisively separated.

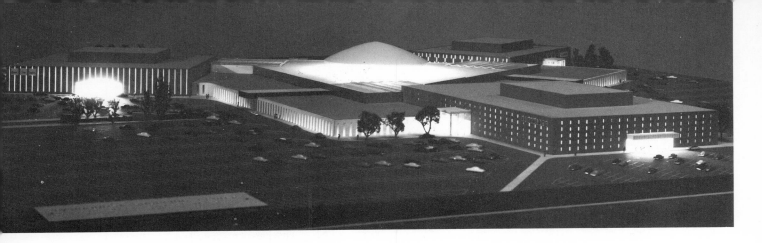

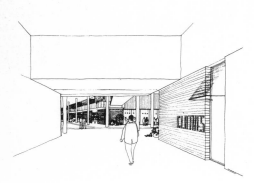

Randhurst is designed to serve a market of 300,000-400,000, north and west of Chicago. This first-of-a-kind shopping center is sponsored by three downtown department stores: Carson Pirie Scott, Wieboldt's and The Fair. The triangular cluster-type scheme—recently completed—revolves about a central, three-level galleria, enclosed by a clerestoried dome of concrete. Victor Gruen Associates, architects: Larry Smith and Company, economic consultants

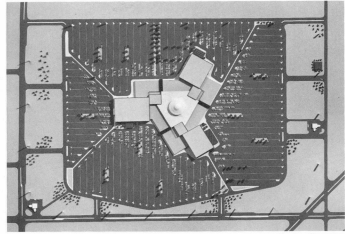

Gordon Sommers

As the automobile flood swelled, the depth of the parking lots had to be increased until it became impossible to construct shopping facilities within the narrow, 150- to 200-ft-deep strips which zoning laws usually allowed for retailing. Thus, special zoning for sites of considerable depth was worked out, and the first shopping centers were born.

Instead of one strip, two parallel strips of stores were built, and parking was arranged outside of both. The space between the strips was made into a pedestrian mall, of minimum width. The merchants, however, still feeling that their best interests were tied to the automobile (that romance again!) gave main emphasis to the store "fronts" facing the parking lots, expecting their customers to park in front of their store and march in by the front door. The mall was underplayed, and considered principally as a short cut for the shopper who desired—after her primary purchase was made—to make secondary visits or purchases in other stores. The mall, long and narrow, featured only a token of "landscaping" in the form of some scraggly little plants, and was altogether empty and dreary. Usually there was a roadway directly adjoining the store groups, based on the idea that people would make short stops along the curb, and also window-shop by driving along the store fronts. This arrangement transferred the congestion and danger of the suburban highway to the roadway along the strips, and I know of at least one such shopping center where traffic signals finally had to be set up on the road between parking lots and stores so that one

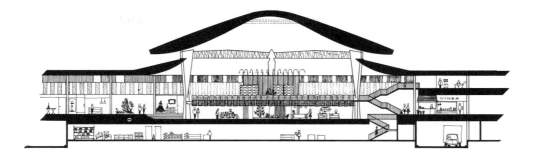

Gordon Sommers

could walk from his car to the stores without endangering his life.

But as merchants, planners, and developers gained experience and wisdom, they realized that shopping activity can be most successfully and pleasantly carried out by people who are on foot and who can concentrate on shopping without being distracted by the dangers, inconveniences, and nervous tensions mechanized traffic brings. Separation of motorized and pedestrian areas became increasingly stringent; service traffic was sent underground.

The hypothesis that dozens of people could park in front of a specific store was abandoned; store entrances facing parking areas became less important; and pedestrian areas were made larger, wider, and more attractive. To an increasing degree, regional shopping centers emulated the ideals of a truly urban crystallization point, and included within their boundaries office buildings, medical buildings, hotels, auditoriums, exhibit areas, theaters, social meeting places, clubs, and facilities for other cultural, recreational, and civic activities.

In addition, the size and shape and variety of pedestrian areas developed; the one narrow mall—reminiscent of Main Street—was replaced by more intricate systems of open, interconnected spaces of various sizes, proportions, and character. These are now called malls, courts, arcades, plazas, etc.

Thus, the well planned regional shopping center came to resemble more and more an historic urban center. And as such centers grew, so did the realization that public transportation could add meas-

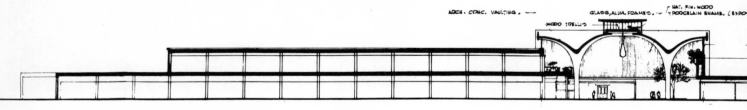

urably to their business; many centers (Northland, Old Orchard, Southdale, Roosevelt Field) have encouraged bus transportation through special roads, bus terminals with waiting rooms, etc.

Where climatic conditions were unfavorable, planners went further: pedestrian areas were enclosed, and by means of air conditioning, special lighting, acoustical control, etc., furnished a pleasant, year-around environment for shoppers. Again, an historic pattern was imitated: the colonnades, galleries, and covered arcades of European cities found contemporary expression in the covered mall.

Thus, the best regional centers are incorporating the best qualities urban centers once had. They can

rightly be regarded as a serious threat to existing downtown centers, which today are lacking in the best urban characteristics, due to lack of foresighted planning. In 1954, I stated (in a *Harvard Business Review* article) that the evolution of the regional shopping center could have two potential effects on those concerned with downtown: first, that of a shock treatment that might stir city officials and business men into action; and second, that of serving as an experimental workshop in which ideas for downtown revitalization might be developed. I feel justified in those statements today. The shock has set in, and action—though in many cases hesitant and misdirected—is at last being taken (or at least it is being planned) in many of our cities.

THE COVERED MALL

Directly across the Delaware River from Philadelphia and 4 miles east of Camden, N. J., the Cherry Hill Shopping Center serves approximately 400,000 people (see page 164). The design focuses on an enclosed, two-level, air conditioned garden street, shown at left. A typical arcade leading to the central area is shown above; a section through the entire building below. Shops are enclosed by sliding doors, left open during business hours for maximum visual recognition. Victor Gruen Associates are architects for the development, jointly sponsored by Strawbridge and Clothier and Community Research & Development, Inc.

The Lederer de Paris shop on Fifth Avenue in New York, built in the early 30's, was an early classic in small shop design that set up new basic principles of styling for retailing still valid today. Morris Ketchum, architect; Victor Gruen, designer

Ewing Galloway

Left: The Lloyd Center, Portland, Ore., designed by John Graham & Co. Above: Rockefeller Plaza, New York, a well known early example of an urban shopping center

John Todd Photo Service

The new downtown pedestrian mall in Kalamazoo, Mich.; landscaping by Nicholas Kik

The Bettmann Archive

View of the medieval (and contemporary) market square in downtown Leipzig, Germany

Urban Shopping Centers

A new kind of shopping center has appeared; the urban shopping center, in which the downtown area—father of all commercial centers—translates lessons learned from the suburban children into the downtown vernacular.

The Lloyd Center in Portland, Oregon, designed by John Graham, is an example. Located near the center of the metropolitan population, and only a few miles from the existing business center, it includes office buildings, hotels, institutional buildings, and other typical downtown elements. Service traffic is underground and vehicles are excluded from pedestrian areas, which are of various sizes and shapes. Since the Lloyd Center occupies expensive urban land, parking is in multi-level garages, and

public transportation facilities are also provided.

Our own office has designed an urban shopping center, Midtown Plaza, which is located in the heart of downtown Rochester, New York. It includes two department stores and fifty smaller stores, plus a new hotel which is Rochester's largest, a high-rise office building, auditorium, recreational facilities, etc., all arranged about a protected pedestrian area which was formerly a busy, downtown vehicular thoroughfare. Some of the structures are existing downtown buildings (a cinema, for example, is connected by underground passage to a three-level, 2,000-car garage beneath the entire development), while certain others are new. From all levels of the garage, one can ascend by escalator to the pedestrian mall, which will be cov-

Rochester (N.Y.) Democrat & Chronicle

This photo of the lively and well-attended "Ball In The Mall" offers evidence that a downtown renaissance is indeed under way in Rochester, N. Y., and that the community is making full use of its new urban center, Midtown Plaza, as architect Victor Gruen intended

ered and air conditioned. Pedestrians may stroll in a space defined by variously shaped elements (the largest of which rises two stories) to create the character of a restful and attractive garden court with planting, flowers, fountains, sculpture, and benches. A new bus terminal within the center serves out-of-town, suburban, and city lines; additional bus stops are provided at various points on the perimeter.

Another multi-purpose, urban shopping center now being built is Westchester Plaza, in downtown New Rochelle, New York. It will be located only two blocks from the present business center, and will be built over the tracks of the New Haven Railroad. It will include a railroad terminal and ticket offices, as well as a bus terminal, multi-deck parking for 5,000 cars,

an auditorium, an office building, a hotel, and about one million sq ft of retailing space. It will be a high-rise building with five parking levels, two merchandising levels, 12 floors of offices, and a 100-room hotel. The majority of the stores can be reached only from the air-conditioned mall. Escalators and elevators from parking decks, railroad platforms, and bus terminals will carry shoppers to the pedestrian mall.

The foregoing three projects have one quality in common which accents the difference between urban and suburban shopping centers; they occupy much less land. Westchester Plaza—if built on cheap suburban land—would cover about 100 acres. On urban land, however, it will occupy only 19 acres. Midtown Plaza covers 10 acres.

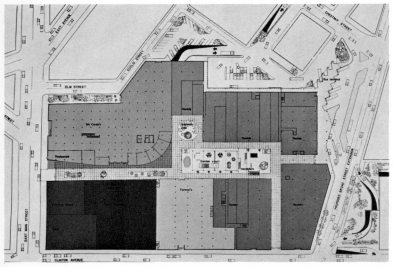

FIRST FLOOR

THE URBAN SHOPPING CENTER

Midtown Plaza, Rochester, N. Y., is the nation's first downtown urban renewal shopping complex to be completed. Initiated under private sponsorship (two department stores), the project covers 10 acres in the heart of downtown Rochester. It includes: two department stores; an air-conditioned, two-level mall lined with 50 stores; a three-level underground parking garage for 2,000 cars; and an 18-story high-rise building housing stores, offices, a three-floor hotel, and a restaurant. The section below shows the main elements of the project, designed by Victor Gruen Associates, with Larry Smith & Co. as economics consultants and Ladislas Segoe as planning consultant to the City of Rochester

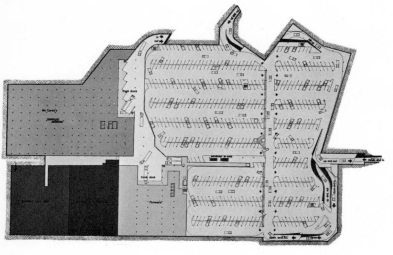

PARKING LEVEL

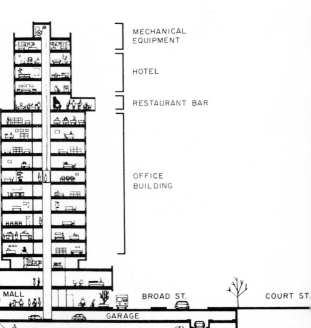

MECHANICAL EQUIPMENT

HOTEL

RESTAURANT BAR

OFFICE BUILDING

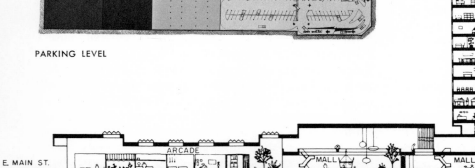

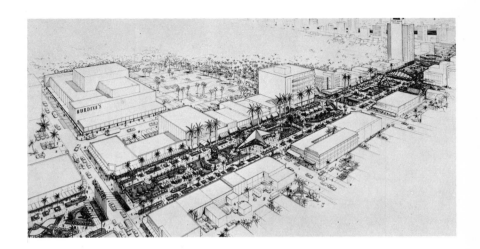

Design to convert palm-lined, 100-ft-wide Lincoln Road in Miami Beach into an attractively landscaped pedestrian mall. The project, designed by architects Morris Lapidus, Kornblath, Harle & O'Mara, will be maintained by the city as a park

Downtown Revitalization

The core area of our cities has—in the large majority of cases—one inherent advantage suburban centers can never possess. It is located in the midst of an urban region about which the largest buyer's market centers. Despite the prophets of gloom, if full advantage of this potential is taken, downtown will become once more the most dynamic and economically sound retail, business, cultural, and administrative center of its region. But, downtown will have to do much more than it now does. One-way avenues, arterial highways, municipal parking, widening of streets, and downtown promotions of various types will not do the trick, and serve only as temporary expedients. The present rash of downtown malls serves only to demonstrate the desire of shoppers for a quieter, safer, more restful environ-

ment. But since most of the mall experiments are limited in scope and executed without regard for basic requirements (access, parking, services, etc.) they must be regarded as merely another promotion.

Downtown revitalization must be based on a clear over-all concept embracing all the qualities that make an urban environment both attractive and economically sound. Our plan of four years ago for downtown Fort Worth points in this direction. In developing it, we first delineated and defined the area which should be regarded as the core of the city. We tabulated present land uses and confronted this list with a tabulation of desirable land uses for the next twenty years. The comparison showed that the desired compactness could not be achieved at present because many low productivity land uses

111

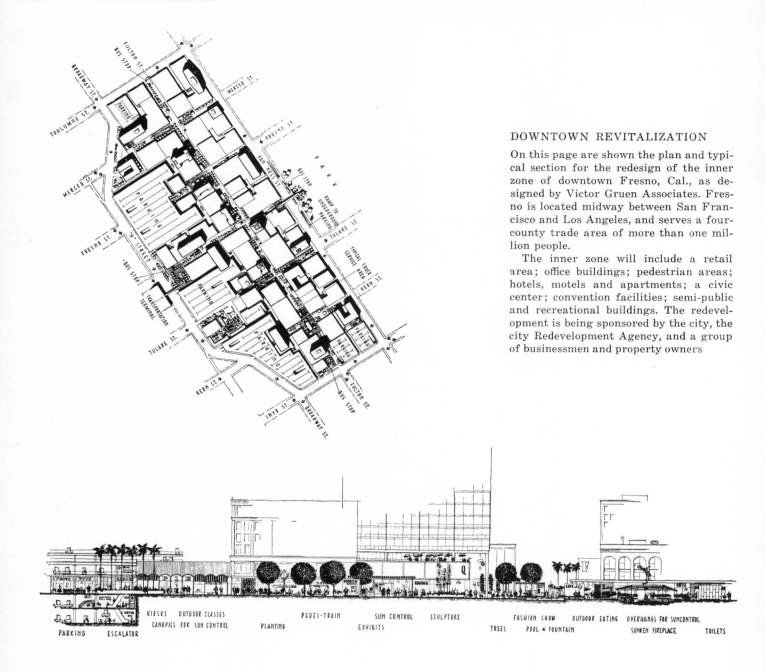

PARKING ESCALATOR KIOSKS OUTDOOR CLASSES PEDES-TRAIN SUN CONTROL SCULPTURE FASHION SHOW OUTDOOR EATING OVERHANGS FOR SUNCONTROL
CANOPIES FOR SUN CONTROL PLANTING EXHIBITS TREES POOL & FOUNTAIN SUNKEN FIREPLACE TOILETS

DOWNTOWN REVITALIZATION

On this page are shown the plan and typical section for the redesign of the inner zone of downtown Fresno, Cal., as designed by Victor Gruen Associates. Fresno is located midway between San Francisco and Los Angeles, and serves a four-county trade area of more than one million people.

The inner zone will include a retail area; office buildings; pedestrian areas; hotels, motels and apartments; a civic center; convention facilities; semi-public and recreational buildings. The redevelopment is being sponsored by the city, the city Redevelopment Agency, and a group of businessmen and property owners

(storage, warehousing, manufacturing, and particularly the handling of moving or parked vehicles) interfered with the homogeneity essential to the functioning and practicability of a true urban center. Excluding all these non-compatible land uses, we then delineated a compact core area which would provide ample space for all compatible downtown uses and also those which could be expected to grow; plus generous open spaces, plazas, squares, and parks. This area was so compact it proved practical to make it a single pedestrian area, only slightly larger in size than several of the large regional shopping centers.

The plan called for an inner multi-lane loop road tightly circling the core area, into which highways from all directions would terminate. Adjoining this road, six multi-story parking garages were designed to provide 60,000 parking spaces. These rectangular garages will have their short sides on the loop road and their long sides reaching like fingers into the core area. Thus, no vehicular entrance will be more than two to two and one-half minutes walking distance from the central point of the pedestrian area. Special bus roads run along the sides of the garages; terminals are located near the center of the core area. Special arrangements were made for service and emergency traffic.

Monotony is avoided by variety in the shaping of open spaces. In certain areas we propose covered pedestrian spaces, especially where high density retailing occurs. The environment will be visually enhanced and made more convenient by colonnades

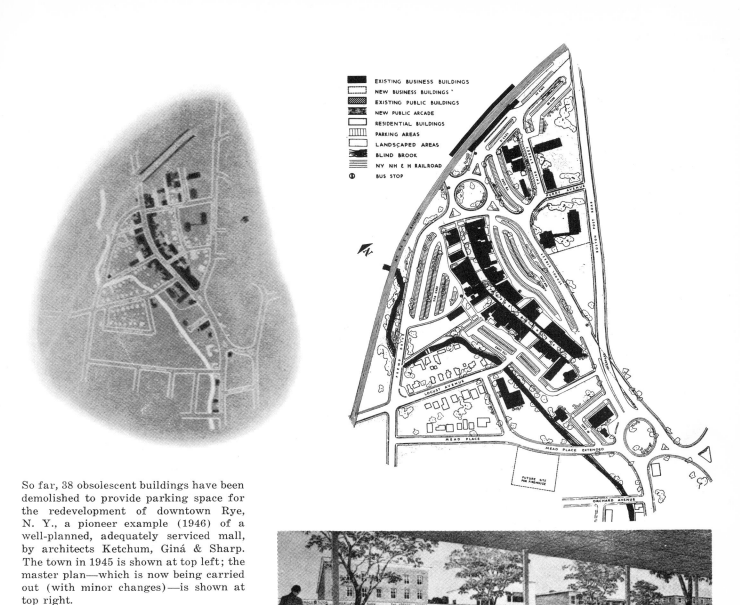

So far, 38 obsolescent buildings have been demolished to provide parking space for the redevelopment of downtown Rye, N. Y., a pioneer example (1946) of a well-planned, adequately serviced mall, by architects Ketchum, Giná & Sharp. The town in 1945 is shown at top left; the master plan—which is now being carried out (with minor changes)—is shown at top right.

Architect Morris Ketchum says, "The temporary mall idea is doomed to failure unless preliminary plans include proper provisions for perimeter traffic, automobile access, and adequate parking. You can't have all icing and no cake"

and other sidewalk shelters, covered crosswalks, landscaping, benches, fountains, sculpture, murals, exhibit areas, sidewalk cafes, etc.

The principles used in the Fort Worth plan have been followed more or less ably in master planning projects for about 50 cities.

If and when plans for city cores (now in various stages of preparation) are realized, urban shopping centers will rise to new importance. However, to think this will spell the end of suburban shopping centers is fallacious, for they will continue to play their specific role in meeting marketing and other needs, and to a lesser degree shopping-goods requirements. For the large cities, they will become satellite centers for shopping, cultural, social, and recreational needs.

The same planning principles apply to both urban and suburban centers, modified only by the fact that suburban land is cheaper and more easily available, and that mass transportation must play a larger part in the urban center, regardless of size or type. Most merchants fail to realize that the same principles apply to both, and downtown retailers—faced in most cities by an alarming drop in volume—think their salvation lies in more automobile traffic and more parking garages near their stores. They still fail to transfer their attachment from the automobile to the shopper, and are aided and abetted in their demand for more traffic by many traffic experts and city planners: Mr. Wiley, ex-head of New York's traffic department, stated, "I have yet to see a city choked to death because of too much traffic. Cities

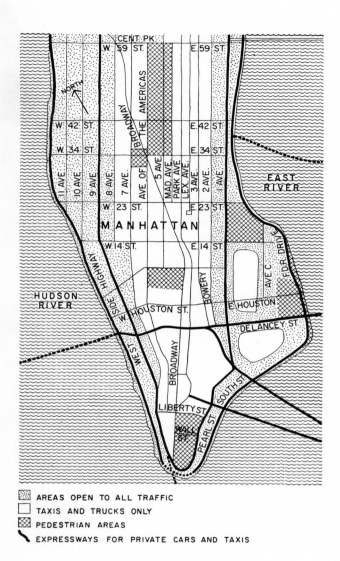

☒ AREAS OPEN TO ALL TRAFFIC
☐ TAXIS AND TRUCKS ONLY
☒ PEDESTRIAN AREAS
❮ EXPRESSWAYS FOR PRIVATE CARS AND TAXIS

HOW ABOUT ZONING
FOR MANHATTAN TRAFFIC?

Victor Gruen says, "When asked if my approach to urban redevelopment could be applied to Manhattan, my answer (published in *The New York Times Magazine* on Sunday, January 10, 1960, proposes this basic idea:

"Zoning, which presently applies only to buildings, should be extended to cover the entire land mass of the city, including transportation. Areas not presently zoned (roads, parking lots, parking garages, etc.) occupy about one third of the total area in Manhattan, in the most urbanized of all cities.

"Zoning categories would then be set up for all areas, such as: zones for foot traffic only; for surface public transportation; for taxis only; for vehicular services (garages, etc.). Emergency vehicles could go anywhere; special arrangements might be made—if desirable—to permit service traffic in certain zones during carefully limited hours.

"If one applied such a scheme, then he could visualize an express traffic zone beyond the present one (West Side Highway and East River Drive) and located two or three blocks from each river. Accessory automobile zoning could then be spotted in the area between the two express zones and immediately adjoining the inner express loop, on a narrow strip. The remaining central area would then be zoned for public and semi-public transportation only (busses and taxis), with two exceptions: streets specifically semi-industrial (as the garment center) might be zoned for service traffic exclusively; and the highly qualified retail, office zoned for foot traffic only. Thus Fifth Avenue from 42nd to 59th Streets (together with certain side streets and Herald Square) could be converted into an attractive pedestrian island. Likewise, the Wall Street area and certain residential communities could be made strictly pedestrian oases"

expire because they don't have enough traffic, and we . . . say we serve as much traffic as we can."

Mr. Wiley's trouble is that he has hypnotized himself into believing that there is only one type of traffic—motor vehicles. And for this, he is willing to sacrifice public transportation, which today takes care of 80 per cent of all Manhattan-bound persons during rush hours; he is willing to cripple pedestrian traffic, and if pressed to the wall by the rising flood of cars, might want to sacrifice all the buildings in the city! He forgets—as most traffic engineers do —that traffic is a means of travel, not an end in itself. Our aim should be to move as many *people* and as much *merchandise* as possible, not to move as many *vehicles* as possible through streets flanked by buildings which are thus made unsuitable for human

activity. The sensible approach would utilize the most efficient carriers in such a way that they do not interfere with each other or with people on foot.

Thus, both in suburbia and downtown, we see the romance slowly ending; and find it being replaced by a more sensible and more lasting marriage based on convenience. Convenience for the automobile, in surroundings best fitted to its technological potentials—freeways and expressways where it can safely develop its speed; convenience and prosperity for the retailer, by giving him the true object of his affection—the shopper on foot, unharried by traffic—in an environment which is safe, pleasant, and also good to look at.

Above: Whirling Dervishes—6-ft metal sculpture by Nathaniel Kaz. *At right:* mall next to the Federal department store; glazed brick mural by Richard Jennings

FESTIVE ATMOSPHERE HELPS SALES

WONDERLAND REGIONAL SHOPPING CENTER
LIVONIA, MICHIGAN

by Louis G. Redstone, A.I.A.

A basic design goal for this center was to bring about a festive and colorful environment; to create a marketplace that would make shopping a gayer, more interesting experience set in sprightly, good-natured, attractive surroundings. Merchandising experts tell us that dollars come out of womens' purses more readily in such an atmosphere; and return visits will of course be more frequent when the center has the power to amuse or attract both children and grownups. In carrying out this concept, two factors played a large role: the proportions, scale, and character of the malls and sheltered crosswalks; and the extensive use of the related arts, i.e., mural decoration, sculpture, planting, fountains, graphics, etc. The fact that many people visit the center for browsing as well as shopping—even on Sundays, when stores are closed—proves the validity of the idea. Wonderland may well emerge as the center for a wide variety of social and recreational activities in the area, and may soon become an important hub of the city. A recreational center and professional offices for the center are now in preliminary design.

The Rooster—6-ft metal sculpture by Donald Buby

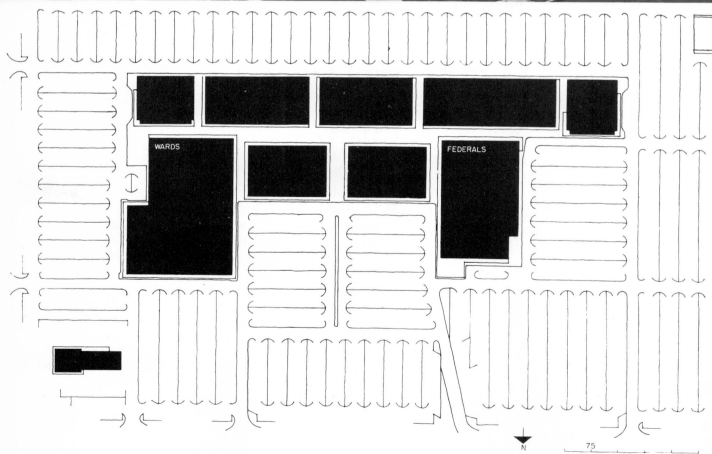

ARCHITECTS: *Louis G. Redstone; Avner Naggar, Associate Architect; The late Allan G. Agree, Associate Architect*

Participating Staff: *Bernard W. Colton, Coordinator; Samuel Hack, Mechanical; Albert E. Lawrence, Structural*

LANDSCAPE ARCHITECTS: *Eichstedt-Johnson Associates*

CONTRACTORS: *Walter L. Couse & Co., General Work; Perron Construction Co., Montgomery Ward store*

Mall near Federal department store

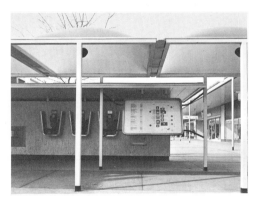

The Orientation Center

Shaped landscaped areas in main mall

The Plan

The plan is based on the idea of a magnet, or anchor, at each end of the complex. The two principal tenants, Montgomery Ward and the Federal Department Store, occupy the anchor positions. Added interest and strength is given to the Federal portion of the plan by the introduction of an arcade building, which provides space for various service and specialty stores such as barber, beauty shop, shoe repair, flower shop, etc. This building also houses the auditorium and the center's offices.

In order to attract the shopper to other tenants, a "T" shaped main mall was introduced leading the shopper past these stores, before proceeding to either of the major department stores. This "T" mall is visually extended into the main parking area through a covered landscaped walk. Added directional incentive was gained by reversing the parking pattern perpendicular to the walk. This walk originates at the "Spike", a 75 ft steel landmark dominating the main approach.

Shopping Environment: The Malls

In the search for proper scale and a comfortable shopping environment in the malls, the open spaces between buildings were very carefully studied. The width of 64 ft for the main "T" mall gives the shop-

per the proper feeling of intimacy, not so large that he loses identity, yet wide enough for effective commercial displays. The narrower 30 and 40 ft malls opposed to the interplay of solid walls versus canopied fronts creates effective visual contrasts. The proportions of the malls were studied in relation to building heights; spatial divisions were defined by cross-overs, orientation shelters and landscaped area. The result is a changing series of visual experiences, in size, in shape, in color, in material, in texture, etc., adding up to an exciting shopping atmosphere.

The cross-overs, built of steel and plexiglass domes, accent with different colors the various mall locations, helping the shopper to orient himself. The colorful glow of the domes at night harmonizes with the soft lighting from the column lanterns. During the day the rhythmic pattern of the white lanterns is reflected against the curved polished shapes of the domes.

The interest of the shopper is also subtly carried to the pattern of the mall walks. The paving patterns are done in black and light grey concrete with linear accents of black terrazzo-like asphalt paving blocks.

Colorful landscaped areas and fountains soften all malls and complement the organized paving pat-

Main mall looking west toward Federal store. Fountain by Richard Jennings

Concrete and ceramic Laughing Horse, by Rosemary Zwick

Main entrance mall next to parking

42 ft mall at Montgomery Ward store

Whirling Dervishes by Nathan Kaz in mall location

Fountain by Richard Jennings

Precast concrete mural, Marjorie Kreilick, sculptress

Family of Bugs,
by Betty Conn

tern; their impact is heightened by the variation in size, shape and height.

Shopping Environment: Art

An important factor contributing to the festive and interesting environment is the introduction of extensive art work. Two large murals were executed in vivid colors of standard size glazed bricks: one 80 ft long by 10 ft high, designed by Richard Jennings, depicting animal and plant forms derived from temperate and tropic zones. The intricate pattern includes elephants, snakes, giraffes, an octopus, etc. The other brick mural, by Gerry Kavanaugh, depicts a colorful landscape of flowers and foliage. The bricklayers followed the pattern to the minutest detail, proving that brick has many uses. This skilled brickwork also brings together the artisan, artist and architect and belies the opinion that there are no dedicated craftsmen in this country. Another abstract mural 120 ft long, designed by Marjorie Kreilick, was executed in precast concrete panels and chipped aggregates; each panel 3 ft by 12 ft was prefabricated in the shop from full size patterns by the artist.

In the walks through the malls there are many other pleasurable and amusing experiences for the shopper: the "Whirling Dervishes", designed by Nathan Kaz, a pair of 6 ft figures rotating slowly on their base; three fountains, each having its own unique character, designed by Samuel Cashwan, Richard Jennings and Betty Conn; two whimsical figures—"The Laughing Horse" and the "Cat" —by Rosemary Zwick, made of concrete with inlaid ceramics; and a 6 ft "Rooster" by Donald Buby, with colorful enameled metal feathers and tail.

Color and visual interest is also carried into the parking area through the use of graphics. Parking areas are identified by signs mounted on lighting poles. These signs graphically illustrate various animals, flowers and other geometric figures, their colors and shapes making it easy for the shopper to locate his parked car.

Service

Of vital importance to the Center is ease and convenience of merchandise delivery, especially for the smaller stores with limited sales staff. Three main types of servicing were considered: the full underground service, the courtyard service, and direct surface service.

The underground service system was discarded because of its prohibitive construction and maintenance costs and its doubtful maximum utilization

PHOTOS on pages 115-120 are by David R. Kitz, John Gaffield Studio, Baltazar Korab, Aurora Photographic and Richard Jennings

Entrance drive identification

Enameled steel parking signs

The Cat, by Rosemary Zwick

by the tenants. The enclosed service court arrangement, with each court serving a group of stores, was quite adaptable, but occupied excessive valuable space and eliminated store frontage.

The introduction of a limited tunnel originating at a central service point, leading to the front and branching out underground to serve the two North buildings, proved very successful. This tunnel is served by an elevator and an inclined conveyor belt. Electric cars within the tunnel carry merchandise to individual tenants.

Structural

Based on economical spans, an orderly gridiron structural steel system was established for the entire Center, with the exception of the Montgomery Ward Store. This was designed in an effort to anticipate the needs of future tenants. To allow for freedom in store front design in unassigned areas, columns were eliminated from all store fronts by setting the columns back 10 ft from the building line. The structural system itself is based on the cantilever beam principle, which lightens the steel sections considerably.

An entirely different solution was used for the structural system of the Montgomery Ward Store. Here the first floor construction was of reinforced concrete, caisson foundation, and concrete waffle ceiling; while the second floor was designed for structural steel framing.

Dual Ownership

The dual ownership of the Center provided a challenge which appeared in the very preliminary stages of development. While the major department store—Montgomery Ward & Co.—owned its land and building, the balance of the Center was built by a developer for leasing to individual merchants. This factor required initiative and firm control on the part of the architects in the establishment of project requirements which would be binding for all tenants.

The ultimate goal was to create continuity of architectural design and a unified character for the entire complex. However, the tenants' individual identity was retained and expressed within the overall pattern. Heights of buildings and canopies, use of materials, location of services, size and placement of signs and an overall color scheme, all contributed to the unification of the Center.

Serving more than a dozen communities, Wonderland occupies 60 acres, with an additional 20 acres set aside for expansion. The center is located midway between Detroit and Ann Arbor, Michigan.

AMERICA'S LARGEST SHOPPING CENTER

There is interesting variety within a skillfully organized, dominant architectural pattern at Roosevelt Field. There is an assuring, human scale everywhere — not easy in the world's largest center; there is visual intrigue and delight — changing, colorful, but always under control; and there is an ordered, easy-to-learn traffic flow for pedestrian and driver. In short — it's fun to shop here.

Architect I. M. Pei says, "The site plan is essentially a free-flowing ring road surrounding a central building group. The stores form a compact cluster, minimizing walking distances and heightening cumulative drawing power. The relatively narrow malls encourage cross shopping, double the presentation of merchandise, and heighten the impression of activity. The shopper's route leads him through streets of different widths and varying architectural treatments, affording a variety of experiences. Trees, flowers, music, fountains, gay awnings, and bold use of graphic art combine to make the retail atmosphere. Variety of store front design along malls was encouraged.

"Store fronts facing parking areas are designed by the center architect to give the impression of a planned center, yet provide tenant identification. A modular system of dark-brown steel frames, rough-faced off-white brick and glass was used. Within this system, each store was given individual treatment."

Throughout, the structural module is 26 by 32 ft, with the basic 26-ft store front dimension subdivided into 4 parts. Basic heights: inner stores 12 ft; outer stores 16 ft; doors 7 ft. Sign sizes, colors and materials are rigidly controlled.

1—Two variety stores and lower priced-apparel stores, 2—Specialty shops, 3—Quality stores, mainly apparel, 4—Hard goods, housewares, 5—Macy's, 6—Supermarkets, 7—Outdoor skating rink.

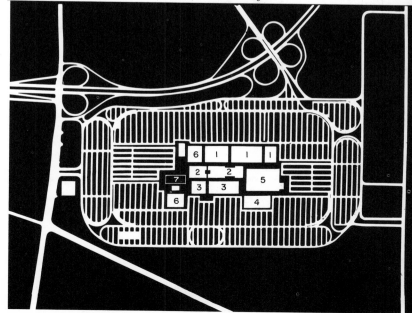

ROOSEVELT FIELD SHOPPING CENTER
Nassau County, Long Island
A Webb & Knapp Project

Architects: I. M. Pei & Associates. Project Staff: O. Aftreth, A. P. Moore, J, LoPinto, A. Candido. Graphics Head: Don Page. Associate Architect: R. C. Brugnoni. General Contractor: George A. Fuller Co.

Consultants: Structural, Severud-Elstad-Krueger; Mechanical, Syska & Hennessy; Special Lighting, H. Abe Feder; Landscape, Robert Zion; Traffic Engineers: Wilbur Smith

1

2

3, 4

5

The Flight Mall, **left page,** extends from Macy's store north to the skating rink. The multi-colored flags were designed by Kenneth Resen, of I. M. Pei's graphics department.

The bus terminal, **1 & 2,** is attractively sheltered by wire glass panels in aluminum extrusion surrounds held by the dark brown steel framework. The architect's graphics men designed the parking identifiers in varying gay colors, **3;** the shopping bag, **4,** with orange balloon, black letters; and the entrance sign, **5,** consisting of 40-in. white plastic globes, inside lighted and with black letters. The 4-in. aluminum tube supports — just erected — will soon have their bases hidden by spreading plants.

All photos © Ezra Stoller, except 3, Dominic Arbitrio and 5, Robert Slutsky

6

7

The Fountain Mall — shown variously in **6, 7, 8,** and on the **left page** — features two types of fountains along its length; the squatty mushroom and the row of high jets. All fountains in the center use a total of 2200 gal. of water per minute, 25 per cent of which passes through diatomaceous filters to be recirculated. In winter, the water is tempered by special heating units. Before final installation, various experimental setups were made in order to study nozzle sizes and flow patterns. For nighttime use there are amber, blue and green underwater lights, controlled by rheostat. The tanks are welded steel construction, painted blue; the curbings are of stone.

8

All photos © Ezra Stoller

9

10

Macy's largest suburban branch, designed by Skidmore, Owings & Merrill, is seen, **10,** through a pattern of weeping cherry trees; and **left page,** flanking the west mall with a typical kiosk in the foreground.

Ten kiosks spotted about the center, **9,** impart a delightful continental touch, and are — or have been — in use for keymakers, pretzel vendors, benefits, Air Force recruiting, and even for automobile insurance!

Electric stairways, **11,** lead to the lower level concourse, where there are 25 additional shops, rest rooms, center administrative offices, a radio broadcasting studio, a 400-seat meeting room for community use, a home building products display center and an art center.

11

All photos © Ezra Stoller

12

13

Typical of all the malls, the Plaza, **left page** and **12,** is paved with sound reducing 9-in. hexagonal asphalt blocks, ground to expose the bluestone aggregate. They serve as the field between divider strips of stone in a modular pattern that aligns with the modular pattern of the buildings.

The Continental Court, **13,** features a fountain with granite curb-bench and restful classical music from hidden sources.

The outdoor skating rink, **14,** was the last element to be added to the complex.

There is a pick-up area for each of the supermarkets, **page 130,** following. The lettering is in primaries, black and white. The curved bench, variously used throughout the center, is precast concrete.

14

All photos © Ezra Stoller

GARDEN SETTING LENDS CHARM TO SUBURBAN CENTER

A gratifying experience awaits the shopper at Old Orchard, for here one will find a center that possesses a personality peculiarly its own — one which is both charming and unusual. As one strolls about he becomes pleasantly aware of a scene that changes refreshingly — he finds change of pace, of scale, of direction, of shape, of surface. Yet underlying all is the basic unity necessary to wholeness. The lure of around-the-corner urges the shopper on, so he sees more merchandise than he otherwise would. Here is clever planning for business and a delightful environment for humans.

The plan has as its center of gravity the Marshall Field & Co. store, with the professional building and The Fair department store as outlying anchors for the additional stores, service establishments, and restaurants. Study of the plan reveals an informal arrangement that provides, between the buildings, a series of spaces that expand and contract; that are sometimes contained but always continuing. One's view is constantly limited, but never confined.

The one-story buildings have structural steel frames on 20 by 40 ft bays, precast lightweight roof slabs, and brick exteriors; the department stores and professional buildings are framed in reinforced concrete on 25 by 25 ft. bays, have floor and roof slabs of poured concrete, and a variety of finishes. There is an underground truck tunnel for Marshall Field & Co. The entire project is air-conditioned. Heating and cooling comes from a central plant; tenants are billed on a unit cost basis.

1—Marshall Field & Co., 2—The Fair, 3—Supermarket, 4—Variety Store, 5—Drug Store, 6—Restaurants, 7—Office Building above, 8—Bus Platform, 9—Specialty Shops

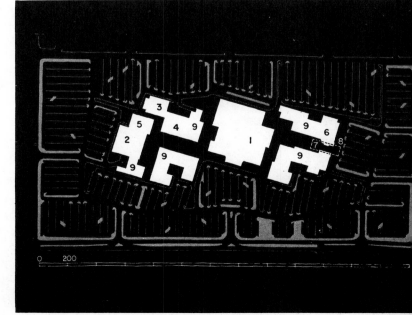

OLD ORCHARD SHOPPING CENTER
Skokie, Illinois
Owner: Old Orchard Business District, Inc.
Rental Agents: Draper & Kramer

Architects: Loebl, Schlossman & Bennett

Consultants: Landscaping, Lawrence Halprin & Associates; Mechanical & Electrical, Robert E. Hattis Engineers; Structural, Alfred Benesch & Associates; Civil Engineering, Joseph A. Schudt & Associates; Traffic Consultants, George Barton; General Contractors, Island Construction Co.

1

2

Principal motor entrances are marked by
the double-O symbol on white painted
brick pylons, **1.** The pylons act as identifiers rather than gates or closures; aid the
driver in finding his way either in or out.

As one enters to the right of the Fair
store, he walks into the mall, **left page,**
leading to the supermarket. A backward
glance, **2,** with the Fair now at right,
shows the fountain marking the turn into
the mall at right angles leading to Marshall Field & Co. The fountain is of concrete and is underwater-lighted at night.

Throughout the center, the various
buildings are linked by covered walkways,
a typical example which is shown in **3.**

3

All photos by Hedrich-Blessing

4

5

Opposite approaches to the Marshall Field & Co. store, **4** and **5,** are interestingly different both in scale and character. Passing through the professional building concourse, one comes upon the intriguing serpentine pool, **left page,** set within a protected court. From the Fair store, **6,** the way is more open, larger in scale.

Though there are two basic building heights, (approximately 9 and 12 ft), one can note — in all the pictures — a pleasing continuity of canopy line throughout the center which serves as a unifying tie. Typical paving is concrete with exposed pebble aggregate, marked by brick strips in a modular pattern that aligns with the building modules.

6

All photos by Hedrich-Blessing

7

8

The various courts adjoining the copper-roofed Marshall Field & Co. first floor, **7, 8, 9,** and **left page,** are charmingly landscaped. Low fieldstone walls form islands in a variety of shapes that serve effectively both to contain planting and to break one's line of travel (see Bennett, **pages 92-94**). The atmosphere here is pleasingly gardenlike and low pressure—but business is good!

The 7-story professional building, **left page,** is surmounted by the center water tank, which is clad in white plastic and which will carry, upon completion, the Old Orchard sign. The spandrels are light-colored brick; the strip fenestration is of fixed aluminum sash; the mechanical shaft is red brick.

9

All photos by Hedrich-Blessing

All photos by R. Wenkam

THIN SHELLS COVER SHOPPING CENTER

NAME: *Windward City Shopping Center*

LOCATION: *Kaneohe, Oahu, Hawaii*

ARCHITECTS: *Wimberly and Cook*

ASSOCIATE ARCHITECT: *George V. Whisenand*

STRUCTURAL ENGINEER: *Richard Bradshaw*

LANDSCAPE ARCHITECT: *George Walters*

CONTRACTOR: *Nordic Construction, Ltd.*

View from the northwest, market is at right, smaller shops beyond

This shopping center derives much of its character from the gay and pleasant way in which reinforced concrete thin shell roofs have been used to enclose each building. This method of structure was selected not only for the playful shapes it offers, but because of lower first costs and minimum maintenance costs. The market (see plan, section and roof diagram on opposite page) is covered by a dome giving an unobstructed area 16,384 ft square. High in the center, the roof overhangs the lower exterior walls and shades the glass areas from the sun. The shape of the dome is a "double torus," segments of two toroid forms at right angles to each other. The radii of the torus arcs are 120 and 240 ft. The dome is supported at four points only by means of concrete buttresses at each corner. The lateral thrust on the buttresses is resisted by means of tie beams along each side from corner to corner. The thickness of the shell varies from 3 in. at the crown to 7 in. near the buttress. Reinforcing over the central section of the dome is a single layer of ½-in. bars running radially and tangentially and spaced at varying distances from 6 in. to 12 in. on center. The other sections of the dome have a double layer of reinforcing gradually increasing in size and density toward the buttresses.

The two other major buildings of the shopping center are divided into many kinds of stores in a variety of sizes. Undulating thin shells on 20-ft square bays form a continuous roof for each structure (see plan and section opposite). The shells are 2 in. thick and are reinforced with ½-in. bars placed 12 in. on center in each direction. No stiffening ribs or beams are needed. The slab is thickened slightly over the column heads.

Unobstructed market interior

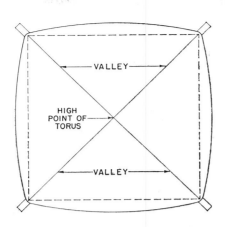

VALLEY

HIGH
POINT OF
TORUS

VALLEY

SECTION

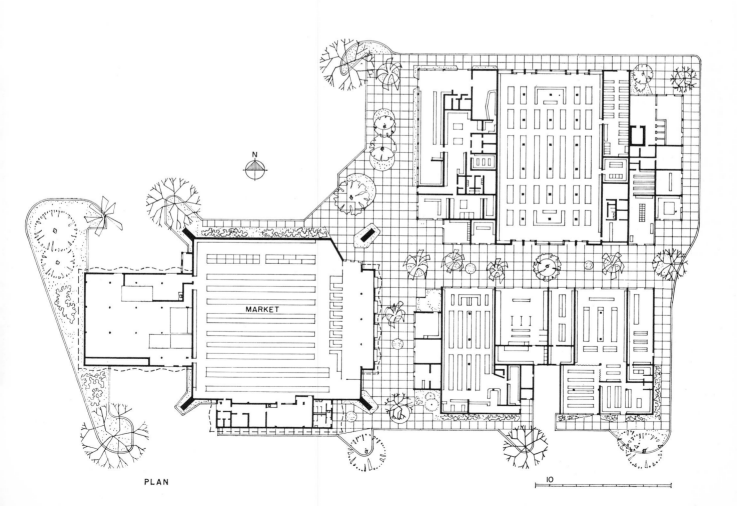

N

MARKET

PLAN

10

Shop fronts consist of aluminum extrusions which hold plate
glass or ¼-in.-thick asbestos board. Exterior filler walls
and interior partitions are non-bearing hollow concrete block

SMALL CENTER KNOWINGLY UNDERSTATED

*Ladera Shopping Center
near Palo Alto, Cal.*

ARCHITECT:
John Carl Warnecke

LANDSCAPE ARCHITECT:
Lawrence Halprin

STRUCTURAL ENGINEERS:
Wildman & Morris

MECHANICAL & ELECTRICAL ENGINEERS:
G. L. Gendler & Associates

The Ladera shopping center skillfully echoes the character of its environment; a high-class residential section which will undoubtedly strive to maintain its pleasantly rural quality as it develops. The center's wide-spreading, wood shingled roofs, its informal grouping of three low buildings, and its almost rustic character—expressed by exposed wood construction with either glass or redwood board-and-batten infilling—all contribute to the effect. The deep shade of the low-hung, sheltering arcades adds an inviting coolness for hot days, as does the fountain (photo next page). All signs were under the control of the architect—except for those stickers supermarket operators insist upon plastering on most of the glass available, and at an angle!

The plan is based on the idea that the shopper is a pedestrian. The three buildings that form the center are grouped in L shape and linked together by covered walks; are oriented to face upon an open, landscaped courtyard that can be reached directly from the parking area.

All photos by Roger Sturtevant

Fountain in courtyard between market and building of shops provides a welcome cooling note

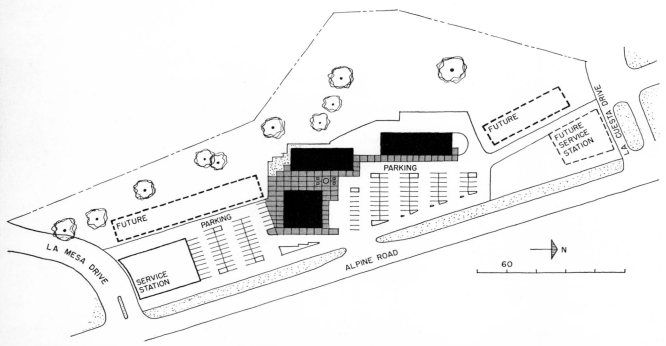

Site plan shows arrangement of the three buildings and parking area on the five-acre plot

View showing the three buildings and their relationship to parking

Looking along the court towards the parking area

Photo showing supermarket in the foreground; parking at the right

CENTER WITHIN A TOTAL SURBURBAN PLAN

Maryvale Shopping City
Phoenix, Arizona

ARCHITECTS:
Victor Gruen Associates

GENERAL CONTRACTOR:
John F. Long Home Builder, Inc.

This handsome shopping center—crisp in form, colorful, and full of visual interest—is actually part of a 6,000-acre total suburban plan (also by Gruen) for the development of a self-contained community of 60,000, located 12 miles northwest of the Phoenix central business district. A notable effort directed against uncontrolled suburban sprawl, the community will eventually include a hospital and medical center, a park, a golf course and club, schools, an industrial park for research and light industry, and housing.

The shopping center consists of five buildings clustered about an interestingly handled garden courtyard, shown in the photo at lower left. The courtyard canopies provide relief from the intense desert sun; some have flat, solid roofs —others are barrell vaulted with special patterned paper embedded in translucent plastic. An arched bridge with tile steps and walk spans a central, T-shaped, dark blue pool which contains groupings of lighting fixtures. The court is variously paved with tile, exposed aggregate concrete with redwood strips, and brick.

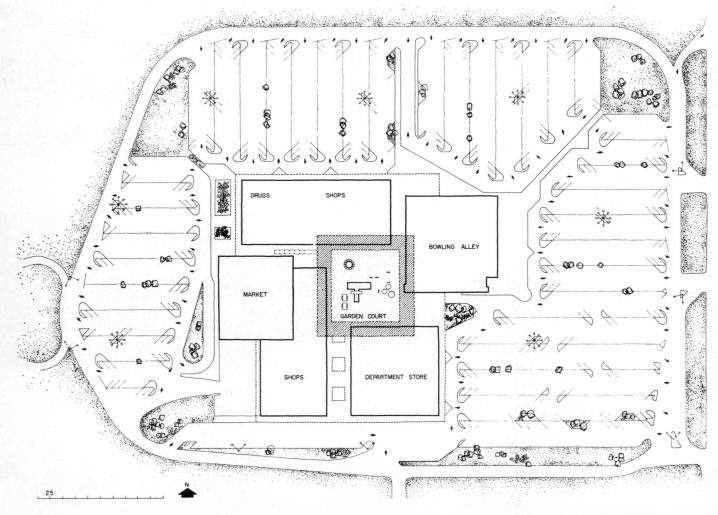

N

© 1961 F. W. Dodge Corporation

Canvas banners with Maryvale symbol mark arcade entrance. Black and white awnings shade a row of shops

Montgomery Ward store has concrete block walls, plaster fascia, metal canopy. Exterior lights make pattern on wall

Bowling alley has block walls painted deep rust color, white plaster canopy with yellow tile panels between beams

Center symbol, derived from Indian symbolism

Parking lot identification markers

Circular signs with desert animal motif identify parking lots

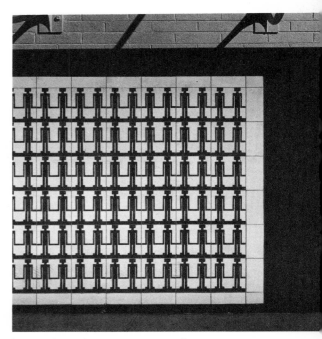

Decorative tile pattern at market entrance

INNER-DIRECTED REGIONAL CENTER

Mayfair Shopping Center
Wauwatosa, Wisconsin

ARCHITECTS:
Perkins & Will and Grassold-Johnson Associates
Marshall Field Store: Loebl, Schlossman & Bennett
Gimbel's Store: Welton Becket & Associates

LANDSCAPE ARCHITECT: *Franz Lipp*

CONTRACTOR: *Hunzinger Co.*

This 20 million dollar shopping center—built on a 150-acre plot in a Milwaukee suburb—is designed with its 70 shops having their main fronts and business entrances opening to an attractive interior mall. The two exceptions to this general principle are the "anchor" department stores, Marshall Field & Co. and Gimbel's which close the plan at the ends. The 960 ft mall is tastefully handled, and with its canopied sidewalks, rest areas, and landscaping, creates an unusually appealing environment for shopping. Fieldstone, white palos verdes stone, concrete, tile, and a wide range of brick and woods are used in various combinations to make a variety of texture, color, and form for visual interest.

The six-story professional office building adds a vertical element to the composition and offers a contrast to the wood and stone of the shops. Its two end walls are of white concrete, while the long façades are curtain walls of aluminum with panels of light blue procelain enamel on steel alternating with the glass in checkerboard pattern.

The center is serviced by a two-lane underground tunnel in loop shape, which can be entered from either of two entrances. The tunnel serves also to carry heat, light, power, and air-conditioning runs for the various stores.

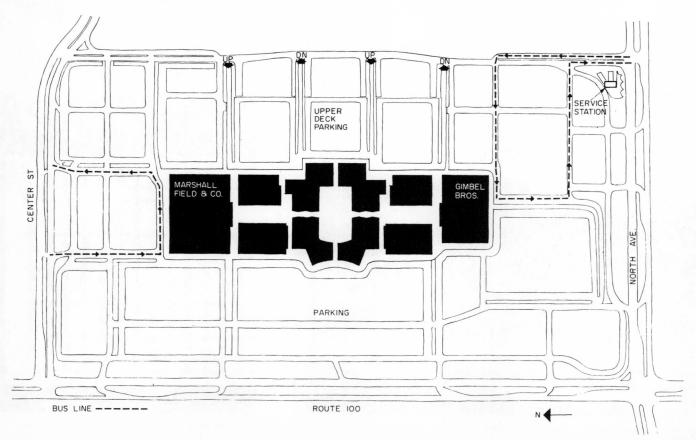

BUS LINE -------   ROUTE 100   N

Two views of the attractively landscaped central mall

The office building strikes a vertical note in the group

Arcaded walks with interesting light and shade

Parking entrance to the Marshall Field store

Lower level entrance to the service tunnel

SHOPPING CENTER FOR CHICAGO RENEWAL

Shopping Center in the Hyde Park Redevelopment,
Projects A and B, Chicago, Illinois

ASSOCIATED ARCHITECTS: *I. M. Pei & Associates*
  Harry Weese & Associates
  Lowenberg & Lowenberg

DEVELOPER: *Webb & Knapp, Inc.*

STRUCTURAL ENGINEER: *Frank Kornacker*

MECHANICAL ENGINEER: *Samuel Lewis*

CONTRACTOR: *Inland Construction Co.*

DIRECTOR OF THE CHICAGO LAND CLEARANCE COMMISSION:
  Philip Doyle

This project was designed and built as an element in the Webb & Knapp portion of the 900-acre Hyde Park-Kenwood urban renewal program in Chicago. Although it is physically separated from residential areas, it is integrated into the planning of surrounding neighborhoods.

Of its design, architect Harry Weese says, "The center was in large part constructed before it was leased, and the drive to reduce building cost brought the parapet down to 3 ft, exposing more roofscape than I felt desirable. In addition, mechanical penthouses were not forbidden, nor rent charged for the ones that were built!

"The basic design consists of 12-ft columns, freestanding, to make non-modular partitioning by tenants possible. The window heads were scaled down to door height to calm the view, so often dominated by fluorescent fixtures and the innards of the stores. The band between the 7- and 9-ft points, where the brick begins, is for signs. Freestanding, thin-shell concrete canopies shade the sidewalks, and serve also to conceal cooling towers for the boutiques. Special attention was paid to scale."

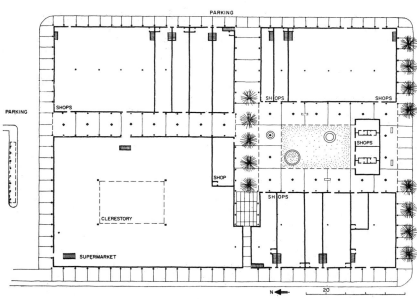

Morley Baer photos

SMALL CENTER
FOR AN UNUSUAL
WEST COAST TOWN

Concerning an appropriate character for this downtown center in Carmel, California, and how it was achieved, architect Olof Dahlstrand says, "The town is largely one of small buildings, which border on the quaint, in a wooded setting on a sandy coast. Therefore, an important aspect of the design was the creation of a scale and feeling compatible with the town. Height was minimized; building elements were held to two stories or less. Variety of forms and the choice of materials within a unifying framework were carefully considered. Materials in character with the surroundings were used, with brick, redwood, and stucco predominate.

"Planting was extensively employed; the several existing trees on the site remain, and were supplemented by a considerable number planted within the project and in adjacent sidewalks. Planting beds and boxes are used on walkways, balconies, arcade areas, overhead trellises, and roofs."

The two photos at left show the side of the center facing the town's principal street (Ocean Avenue). The space between the two major tenants—a bank and branch department store—is devoted to small shops set back to form a courtyard. From this courtyard, a wide walkway with overhead trellis extends through the building to a balcony overlooking the lower level parking area and forested area beyond.

The Carmel Plaza
Carmel, California
OWNER: *The Carmel Plaza Corp.*
ARCHITECT: *Olof Dahlstrand*
STRUCTURAL ENGINEERS: *Carter & Slattery*
MECHANICAL & ELECTRICAL ENGINEERS: *Alexander Boome*
CONTRACTORS: *Stevenson Pacific, Inc., & James I. Barnes Co.*

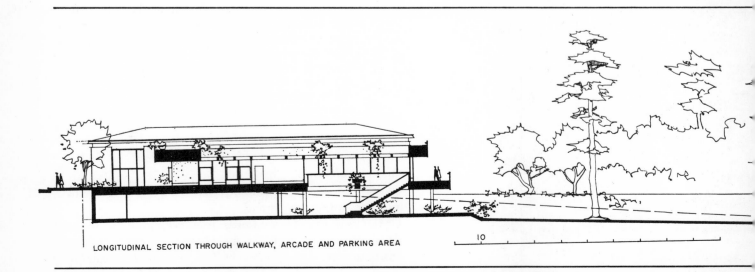

LONGITUDINAL SECTION THROUGH WALKWAY, ARCADE AND PARKING AREA

10

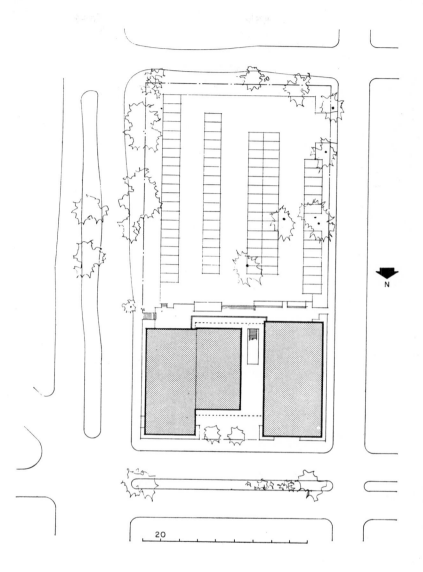

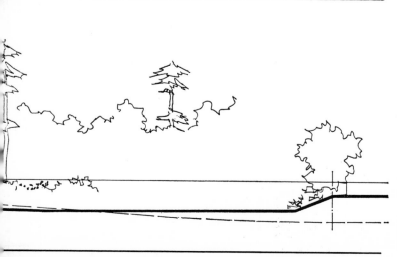

Consideration of the plan, longitudinal section, and photographs on these two pages will make clear the three-dimensional nature of the center, and how it has been arranged to work with the site, which slopes downward 25 ft from front to rear.

The interconnection of the two levels in a manner to encourage traffic between them was an important consideration. From the balcony at upper level, a large (and attractive) open stairway leads down to a lower level arcade of various shops. This arcade leads to a terrace—sheltered by the balcony—which separates building and parking lot. The terrace is set two ft above the parking area to minimize the view of the cars.

Parking is a serious problem in the town, hence provision for parking is an important part of Carmel Plaza. The present parking arrangement is temporary and may be changed [with future development]

ELEGANCE AND RESTRAINT FOR QUALITY TENANTS

The unique character of the Mall shopping center might be summed up in the word *quality*: quality of design, building materials, and construction one does not normally associate with shopping centers; quality of stores and shops—the list of tenants reads like a miniature Fifth Avenue Association; quality of customers from the prosperous suburban countryside nearby. To carry out this idea in visual terms, it was necessary that the architects be in control of store fronts, graphics, and materials; at least for the exterior of all buildings. In typical SOM fashion, all these elements were carefully disciplined and detailed. The result is notable for its unity and dignity. A pattern of uniform column spacing (about 25 ft) was set up, as well as a uniform depth for all stores; a light beige-gray brick was selected for all buildings; all exterior metal work was carried out in aluminum; and great attention was paid to scale in an effort to humanize the whole.

A basic—and difficult—problem was that of integrating the new grouping with an existing B. Altman store on an adjacent eight acres at a higher level. As the photo at left and plot plan on next page show, this was done by neatly shaping the earth to two levels and connecting them with conventional and electric stairways.

The Mall
Short Hills, New Jersey
OWNER: *Prudential Insurance Co.*
ARCHITECTS & ENGINEERS: *Skidmore, Owings & Merrill*
PARTNER IN CHARGE: *William S. Brown*
PARTNER IN CHARGE OF DESIGN: *Roy O. Allen Jr.*
PROJECT MANAGER: *Albert Kennerly*
PROJECT DESIGNER: *Sherwood A. Smith*
MECHANICAL ENGINEERS: *Syska & Hennessy*
GENERAL CONTRACTOR: *John W. Ryan Construction Co.*

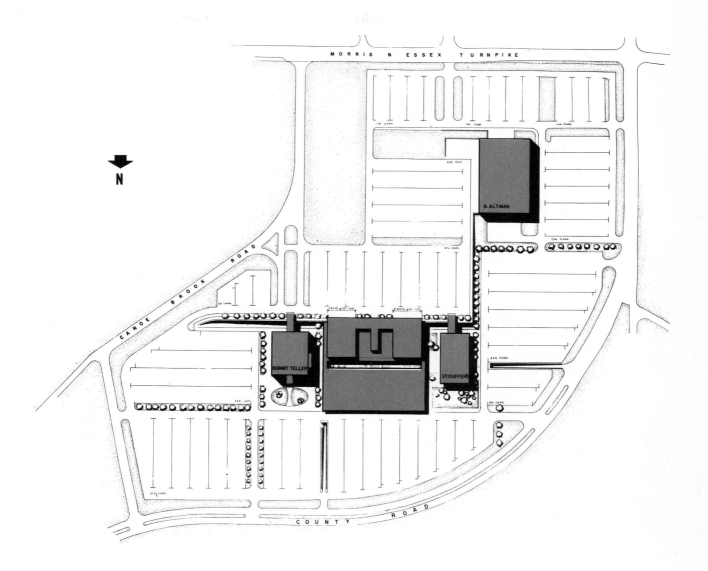

MORRIS & ESSEX TURNPIKE

N

CANOE BROOK ROAD

B. ALTMAN

BONWIT TELLER

STOUFFERS

COUNTY ROAD

The plot plan shows graphically the difficulties involved in integrating the new group of buildings with the existing, five-year old B. Altman building—a distance away and at a higher level. Two distinctly defined levels were created, with parking for each. The concrete retaining wall will soon be ivy-covered and have planting against it for a considerable length. All of the stores in the new group—as well as the restaurant—are serviced from an underground truck tunnel. The restaurant and the three-story Bonwit Teller store rise above the other buildings and are located for visibility from the two highways to the south; see photo at left.

At the outset, the only definite requirement for a master plan was to provide a Bonwit-Teller store, a 25,000 sq ft restaurant, and 300,000 sq ft of space for stores. Then as tenants signed up their spaces were planned within the column spacing [grid]

All photos by Joseph W. Molitor except where otherwise noted

ENCLOSED MALL
WITH AN
OUTDOOR FEELING

Victor Gruen, architect of the Cherry Hill shopping center, says of the design concept, "The underlying purpose of the enclosed mall is to make people feel that they are outdoors—to provide psychological as well as visual contrast and relief from indoor shops —yet at the same time they are provided with the comfort of air conditioning, the chance to sit down and rest a while, and the visual enjoyment of landscaping, fountains, and sculpture." The concept has been skillfully carried out at Cherry Hill, as the photo at left will reveal.

This large center—two department stores, a supermarket, and 75 shops—focuses on a concourse 1,370-ft long, in an L shape, which terminates in three courts, the largest of which, photo at left, adjoins the Strawbridge & Clothier department store. This space, called Cherry Court, is 110 by 172 ft in size, and rises through upward sweeping curves to a skylight 46 ft above the floor. Daylight also reaches this area from clerestory windows in the two side walls. In addition to the fountain, this area includes a Japanese garden, complete with arching bridge and running water, and a fanciful wood gazebo where one may sit and relax.

Cherry Hill Shopping Center
Delaware Township, N. J.
PROJECT ARCHITECTS: *Victor Gruen Associates*
ASSOCIATE ARCHITECTS: *Strawbridge & Clothier Store,*
George M. Ewing Co.
INTERIORS: *Strawbridge & Clothier Store, Welton Becket;*
Food Fair, Kasoff & Bifano;
Cherry Hill Cinema, William Riseman Associates
LANDSCAPE ARCHITECTS: *Lewis J. Clarke*
CONSULTANTS: *Traffic, Wilbur Smith & Associates;*
Real Estate, Larry Smith & Co.

© 1962 F. W. Dodge Corporation

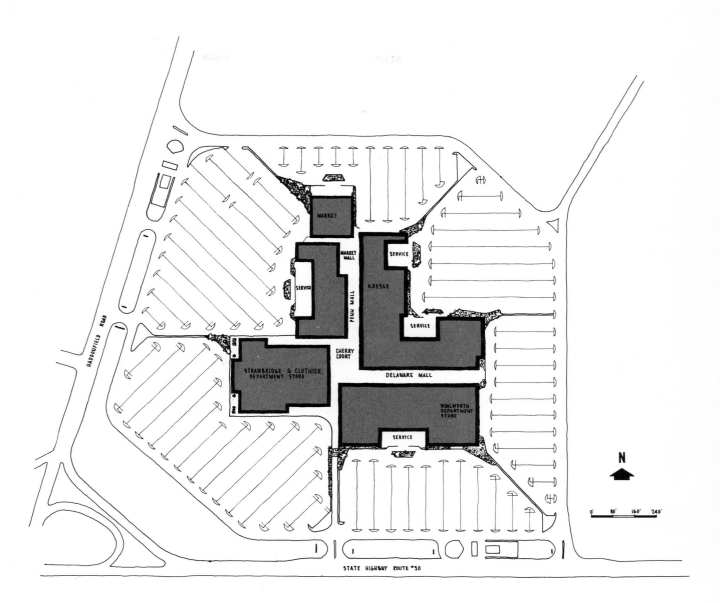

Gordon Sommers

The plot plan above shows the first phase of construction; the rendering at left shows the full extension to the east. The longer mall is flanked by about 12 additional shops and terminates in a court adjacent to Bamberger's department store. The 81-acre site—which devotes 18½ acres to buildings and 62½ acres to parking—is accessible from several directions; offers entrance to the buildings at seven points; and accommodates 6,291 cars. The center is located directly across the Delaware River from Philadelphia, four miles east of Camden, New Jersey, and serves a market of approximately 400,000 people.

The top photo at left shows the exterior (west) entrance to the Strawbridge & Clothier store; the middle photo at left shows the 65-ft wide opening that joins the store to Cherry Court. A restaurant at terrace level overlooks the court

Photos top left show two views looking along Delaware Mall in opposite directions. Constructed as an indoor shopping street 620 ft long, this thoroughfare, which has a 25-ft-high, skylighted ceiling, is lined by 50 stores and a movie theater and terminates in a large court leading to Bamberger's department store. Photo bottom left shows a view of the terrace restaurant overlooking Cherry Court.

There are several ingeniously designed, vertical folding, kiosk shops located in the mid-section of the malls, photo above. Constructed of wood and glass, these small establishments have outer walls composed of showcase and display elements that fold open for daytime business; fold closed for protection at night.

Note, in the two photos next left, how signs for the row of specialty shops and the supermarket have been brought under control. All signs for the center must meet with the architect's approval

Louis Reens photos

BRINGING ORDER
OUT OF MANY
DIVERSE NEEDS

The architect's principal problem in the design of this 31-store center was in reconciling and ordering a diverse set of requirements. The owner demanded maximum sign visibility from the highway, a pleasant arcade, and accommodations for both large and small lessees. The tenants required a variety of store widths and depths (irreconcilable to a standard structural bay); different types of mechanical and electrical systems; store fronts of all types; and various sign requirements of size, height, color, etc.

To organize these diversities, the architects made the linking arcade an expression of steel L-shaped bents on a strictly regular pattern, with all signs supported at the upper level, free of the store fronts, and arcade roofs at low or high levels (for emphasis). Sign panels of uniform height now have the flexibility of different lengths; and have a uniform ivory white background. A system of aluminum store front details was developed to accommodate the various demands of tenants.

The Sears store was conceived as a quiet anchor for the center, yet one strong enough to make a statement amidst the jumpy quality of nearby Route 1 stores. The folded wall is of exposed quartz aggregate precast concrete panels extended above the roof to create a serrated line against the sky.

New England Shopping Center
Saugus, Massachusetts
ARCHITECTS: *The Architects Collaborative,*
Norman Fletcher, Architect in Charge
JOB CAPTAINS: *Shopping Center, William J. Geddis;*
Sears, John Romish
ASSOCIATE ARCHITECT: *Francis X. Gina*
STRUCTURAL ENGINEERS: *Goldberg & Le Messurier*
MECHANICAL & ELECTRICAL ENGINEERS: *Stressenger & Adams*
ELECTRICAL CONSULTANT: *John Maguire*
OWNER-DEVELOPER: *Green Development Corp.*
GENERAL CONTRACTOR: *Vappi Construction Co.*

© 1962 F. W. Dodge Corporation

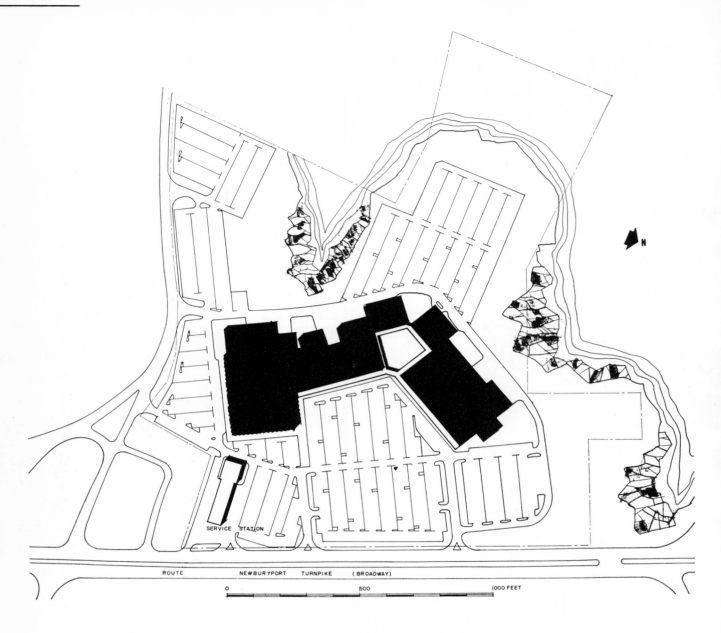

ROUTE   NEWBURYPORT   TURNPIKE   (BROADWAY)

0   500   1000 FEET

The over-all development of the 81-acre site was influenced by the topography and rock outcroppings, which led to a crescent-shaped plan with a court at the junction of the two wings. The future plan includes a third shopping wing to complete the crescent, with Sears as the central anchor. The scheme aims to achieve maximum visual impact from the main highway.

During construction a seasonal sales roof for Sears, photo at left, was requested, and a folded plate shelter in steel was designed. One of the vaults doubles as a parking-lot entrance; natural light enters the shelter through continuous corrugated plastic skylights set into the top plane of the vaults

DESIGN FOR MERCHANDISING

ARCHITECT: *John Graham.* ASSOCIATES (*in office of John Graham*): *Manson O. Bennett, Architect, Manager, Seattle Office; Nathan Wilkinson, Jr., Architect, Project Designer; Alfred H. Fast, Architect, Project Administrator; R. R. Kirkwood, P. E., Director, Mechanical and Electrical Engineering; H. W. Leuschen, P. E., Director, Structural Engineering*

ARTISTS: *Tom Hardy, sculpture; George Tsutakawa, sculpture; Jean Johanson, mosaic; Ray Jensen, sculpture.* CITY PLANNING AND TRAFFIC CONSULTANTS: *Harland Bartholomew and Associates.* ECONOMIC CONSULTANTS: *Larry Smith & Company.* CONTRACTORS: *Donald M. Drake Company; Max J. Kuney Company; Henry M. Mason Company*

All photos by Roger Sturtevant

The design of the Lloyd Center incorporates and re-affirms several sound merchandising principles the architects have proven through their experience in the shopping center field, and the plan comes close to achieving its aim of providing a "100 per cent location" for every store. The merchandising program called for a total of 100 stores: one large department store, one junior department store, and at least two of every other kind of store. The plan is an open-ended T, with the large, four-story department store (C in plan at right) as anchor at the central intersection of stem and cross-bar to serve as the main attraction, or chief traffic "puller." Other stores with strong pulling power (junior department store M, variety stores N, supermarkets T, super drug store S, women's specialty store O, and major shoe store Q) are located at the three ends of the T plan, with parking beyond them minimized. Such an arrangement provides maximum pedestrian traffic for the other stores lining the malls that connect those stores listed above.

Although there had to be three levels (due to the high cost of urban land), the architects have confined nearly all shopping to the mall, or intermediate level, with only supporting merchandising on upper and lower floors; an idea based on recognized retailing practice. The lower level is devoted principally to parking and recreational facilities; the upper level to professional suites and offices. Some of the stores are serviced from above; some from below. Additional parking is variously located on the three levels and in small plots on the periphery of the plan.

The T plan is open-ended in three directions to allow for future expansion, which can be accomplished readily by extending the malls as bridges over intervening streets. Note that every store has both a mall and a "carriage" entrance, so that customers who are so inclined may drive up and park "in front of" a given store and enter from there.

Malls have been held to 50 ft in width (the same as a downtown street) on the basis that a wider space would discourage shopping on both sides. All mall approaches to stores are sheltered by the second floor walkways to the offices overhead.

The Lloyd Center is the largest of its kind, and the first complete urban center. It was conceived as an all-inclusive, 70-acre complex located only six minutes from the old "downtown" Portland—a new commercial nucleus of 100 stores; parking for 8000 cars; a 300-room hotel; an office building; offices within the central group; a skating rink, auditorium, and other cultural and recreational facilities. Additional property owned by the Lloyd Corporation—extending from the center of the Williamette River (see aerial photo, page 173)—will be developed in the future for additional commercial structures, housing, parks, outdoor recreation, etc.

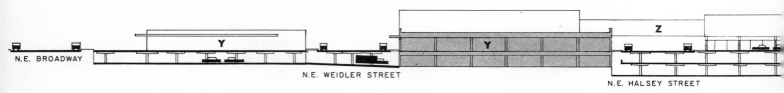

N.E. BROADWAY

N.E. WEIDLER STREET

N.E. HALSEY STREET

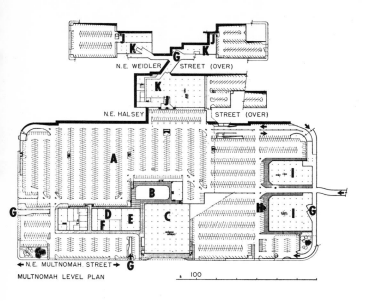

N.E. WEIDLER STREET (OVER)

N.E. HALSEY STREET (OVER)

G ← N.E. MULTNOMAH STREET → G

MULTNOMAH LEVEL PLAN

100

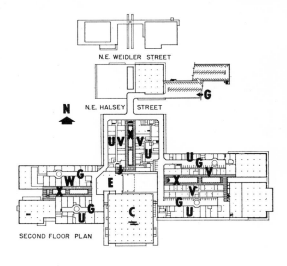

N.E. WEIDLER STREET

N ← N.E. HALSEY STREET

SECOND FLOOR PLAN

LEGEND FOR PLANS
AND SECTION

A. Intermediate parking
   (over)
B. Ice Rink
C. Department Store
D. Auditorium
E. Restaurant
F. Financial Center
G. Service Concourse
H. Elevators
I. Basement Sales
J. Moving Stairs
K. Stock Area
L. East Mall:
   Popular-Priced Stores
M. Junior Department Store
N. Variety Store
O. Women's Specialty Store
P. West Mall: Quality Stores
Q. Major Shoe Store
R. North Mall
S. Super Drug Store
T. Food Market
U. Storage
V. Offices
W. Secondary Shops
X. Mall
Y. Stores
Z. Bridge to Second Floor
   Truck Concourses

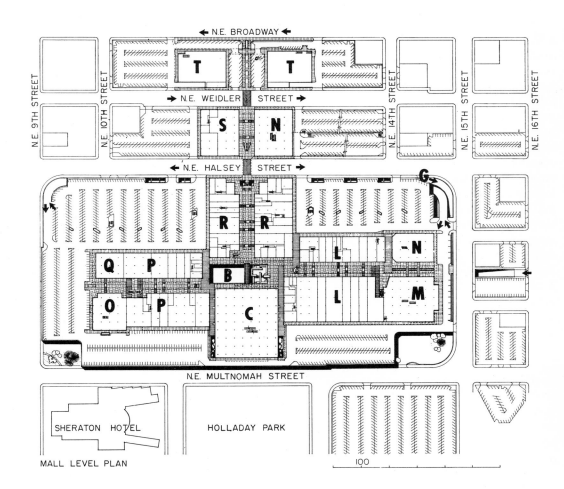

← N.E. BROADWAY →

N.E. 9TH STREET — N.E. 10TH STREET — N.E. 14TH STREET — N.E. 15TH STREET — N.E. 16TH STREET

→ N.E. WEIDLER STREET →

← N.E. HALSEY STREET →

N.E. MULTNOMAH STREET

SHERATON HOTEL — HOLLADAY PARK

MALL LEVEL PLAN

100

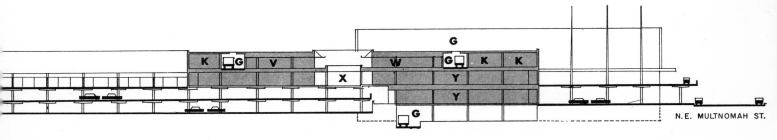

N.E. MULTNOMAH ST.

Graphic design and signs are controlled; landscaping for the malls—in fact for the entire center—will be rotated seasonally (as at Rockefeller Center); fountains, pools, and sculpture enliven open mall areas. The central skating rink—76 by 180—is shown here (two photos at center, left page) in alternate warm weather use as an auditorium. A thin-shell barrel vault roof extending from an upper level restaurant shelters the rink. Sculptor Tom Hardy's bronze "Birds in Flight" is suspended in front of the restaurant windows overlooking the rink.

Parking at Lloyd Center is beside, around, and underneath the stores. A three-level structure is integrated with the store structures, providing covered parking on street and intermediate levels, and outdoor parking at mall level. At some points (as under mall crossings) both covered levels can be seen at once. Cars go from street to intermediate levels on an open ramp. Full size trees and shrubs enhance the small outdoor parking areas.

Unlike so many others, Lloyd Center is not a group of stores in a sea of parked cars. Street views of it are pleasant on all sides, and all are different—for valid reasons. By integrating some parking with the main structure and breaking up outdoor parking into smaller areas, by landscaping its perimeter areas attractively and eliminating garish signs, Lloyd's recognizes a community obligation too often overlooked

Throughout the center planting, water, and sculpture contribute to the environment and are often used to minimize, where possible, the intrusion of essential service or utility elements. Along the East Mall a long opening in the center admits daylight to the entrance driveway (bottom right) for delivery trucks headed for lower level stores (upper level shops receive deliveries in a narrow alley on the second floor with a truck turntable). But strollers on the mall see only the planter boxes (top and bottom left), slightly raised above mall level, which make virtue of the necessary and add color to this dignified, almost austere area. Most unexpected use of sculpture is in the "dry pools" (center) at frequent intervals along the malls. Seattle sculptor Ray Jensen designed these lily pools, herons and fish to stand over the air vents for the parking garage below. Jean Johansen's pebble mosaic pool is a showpiece in the garden plaza

INDEX